Contemporary Mexican Cooking

Gulf Publishing Company
Houston, Texas

Contemporary Mexican Cooking

Famous chefs' recipes for the world's greatest Mexican specialties

Fonda San Miguel • La Esquina • Mansion on Turtle Creek • Matt's Rancho Martinez • Hudson's on the Bend

Via Real • Mesa • La Hacienda • Hokopelli • El Mirador • Boudro's • Bennie Ferrell Catering

Cappy's • Ernesto's • Las Canarias • Mario's and Alberto's • Mark Gonzales • Ninfa's • Z-Tejas

Blue Mesa • Cafe Noche • Casa Rosa • Julia Segovia Ramirez • La Fogata • Los Panchos • Mariano's

Anne Lindsay Greer

Contemporary Mexican Cooking

This is a revised edition. The first edition was published under the title Creative Mexican Cooking. Copyright © 1985 by Anne Lindsay Greer.

Gulf Publishing Company
Book Division
P.O. Box 2608 □ Houston Texas 77252-2608

10 9 8 7 6 5 4 3 2 1

Library of Congress Cataloging-in-Publication Data

Greer, Anne Lindsay.
    Contemporary Mexican cooking / Anne Lindsay Greer.
        p.   cm.
    Rev. ed. of: Creative Mexican cooking. 1985.
    Includes index.
    ISBN 0-87719-273-1(alk. paper)
    1. Mexican American cookery. 2. Cookery, Mexican.
3. Cookery, American—Southwestern style.   I. Greer, Anne
Lindsay. Creative Mexican cooking.   II. Title.
    TX715.2.S69G738   1996
    641.5972—dc20   96-5431
                                                       CIP

Printed on Acid-Free Paper

Printed in Hong Kong

Photographs on pages 12, 58, 94, 108, 124, 152, 176, and 208 are by Greg Milano.

To Jennifer, Gail, and Nancy

CONTENTS

ACKNOWLEDGMENTS

My sincere thanks to all the chefs and restaurateurs who have shared their time, their signature recipes, and their support.

INTRODUCTION

"Tex-Mex" has become the popular catchall word to describe almost any food that has Mexican roots, ingredients, or presentation. If you want a clear definition, don't ask a Texan. He'll shrug his shoulders, give a puzzled look and an elusive answer. Give him a taste, and all the confusion disappears. Despite the differences between the major cities—Austin, San Antonio, Houston, and Dallas—all Texas-style, Tex-Mex food is harmoniously linked to a wider world. Though Texans might not acknowledge it, this is just a piece of a much larger pie. New Mexico, Arizona, and Southern California all have similar roots and a style of food that looks like Tex-Mex, sometimes tastes like Tex-Mex, and is often dubbed Tex-Mex. In the past, regional dishes had clear and well-defined differences; but with the rapid growth of the Southwest and the ever-increasing popularity of its regional foods, the old guidelines and definitions of these foods have become less obvious. The familiar Tex-Mex combination of rice, beans, tacos, and enchiladas remains popular but co-exists with new dishes on a Mexican theme. Traditional Mexican restaurants have expanded to include more grilled meats and seafood, salads, innovative dishes using Mexican ingredients and lighter, contemporary "Southwest Cuisine" items. Enchiladas are no longer limited to fillings of longhorn cheese and chile gravy sauces. Goat cheese, wild mushrooms, seafood, and interesting combinations of fruits and vegetables make up "modern" salsas, tacos, enchiladas, and quesadillas. Chiles are used in creative new ways, and cooking techniques such as smoking, curing, or blackening are applied to tortilla dishes and Mexican ingredients. There is a subtle mix of the old and the new . . . so you might find a mango salsa on an enchilada plate, fajitas made with shrimp or grilled vegetables, and tacos filled with grilled seafood as well as smoked chicken and ground beef. Food critics may recognize the differences between Mexican, Southwestern and Tex-Mex, but to most people who simply want their tacos, enchiladas, and fajitas, the guidelines are less clear and perhaps not important.

Tortilla specialties such as Shrimp Quesadillas or Spicy Swordfish Tacos are typical appetizers on contemporary American menus. Likewise, Duck Taquitos and Fruit Quesadillas pop up in Mexican restaurants. Authentic dishes from the interior of Mexico and their contemporary interpretations are found in restaurants like Cafe Noche in Houston and Fonda San Miguel in Austin. Bill Sadler and chef Allan Mallet were long enchanted with Mexican herbs and the intricate flavors of peppers and spices. Lard and animal fats are reduced or eliminated by these chefs and their counterparts, and new dishes are created from classic Mexican ingredients. Some of these include Cafe Noche's Little Boats de la Noche, in which tenderloin, red snapper, and pork are steamed in tamale husks with a rich adobo sauce or Mark Gonzales' Grilled Swordfish Chile Relleno, stuffed with black beans and corn in a light, richly flavored black bean broth. Boudro's Molasses Cured Salmon Tacos, Blue Mesa's spectacular Adobe Pie, Kokopelli's Blackened Chicken Puff Taco or Chocolate Bread Pudding and Z-Tejas' Voodoo Tuna and Chorizo Stuffed Pork Tenderloin go far beyond the combo platter. Casa Rosa, a Tex-Mex "institution," owned and operated by the El Chico family, serves their Tex-Mex favorites and sizzling fajitas alongside Grilled Goat Cheese Rellenos and Red Snapper Fajitas. How do the customers respond? "They love it" says manager Craig Chug.

Via Real, an upscale Mexican-Southwest restaurant in Las Colinas, follows their signature "chips and salsa" with creations such as Trout Tamale with Roasted Corn Salsa and Squash Enchiladas, reflecting an ever-increasing desire for healthier foods. Cappy Lawton, an enthusiastic aficionado of Mexican food, pottery, and history, peppers his menu with ideas from Mexico and creative specialties such as Southwestern Cobb Salad, Bananas Margarita, or Black Bean Bruschetta at his coffee and juice bar Cappycinos.

As the foods of the Southwest continue to evolve, these innovators and their ideas will continue to be imitated. Mary Trevino's classic Mexican soups at El Mirador have inspired countless versions of Tortilla Soup and Sopa Azteca in Mexican, American and trendy upscale restaurants throughout the country. The PBS television series, *Great Chefs of the West* sought out Mary and others like her, recognizing them as the leaders they are and put their dishes on public television. Jesse Calvillo, who built La Fogata from a drive-in taco stand to the multi-patio, 300-seat restaurant it is today, marries the best of border cooking with traditional Mexican foods. This restaurant has become a standard of regional Tex-Mex food, highly praised by food critics from San Francisco to New York.

Mario Leal opened Chitquitas in Dallas intending to serve the Mexican foods he grew up with, but soon found it necessary to serve Tex-Mex as well. Mario loves to play around in the kitchen and either create something new or work with the chef to develop an idea. "Even if I am at a Chinese restaurant, I may taste something new and try it on my family," he says. Prophetic words, as this is precisely what has happened not only in Texas, but all over the country. These enthusiastic people who love their native foods and ingredients have encouraged a whole new definition of Tex-Mex . . . a delicious blend of Mexican-American border foods, seafood dishes from the Yucatan, modern versions of classic dishes from the interior of Mexico, and vibrant dishes using these flavors and ingredients in exciting new ways.

INGREDIENTS, SHORTCUTS, AND RESTAURANT RECIPES

Restaurant recipes are often difficult to duplicate at home. One reason is that restaurant chefs use homemade stocks as a base for their sauces. Others use a restaurant-supply chicken or beef base, also difficult to find in your local super-market. Smokers, convection ovens, and wood-burning grills add significant flavors to the food, and are difficult to reproduce at home. Fortunately, all the chiles, both fresh and dried, are readily available in most supermarkets from Maine to California. Some of the more unusual items such as blue or red corn tortillas or fresh masa are more difficult to get. Others such as puff taco shells are either time-consuming or messy to make. Homemade stocks, sauces, and beans are a good weekend project that will make the preparation of these recipes much easier.

Many recipes in this book call for roasted poblano chiles and bell peppers or dried chile purees. These may be useful to prepare in large quantities in advance and freeze in small containers. A homemade enchilada sauce is a 5 to 10-minute preparation when you have the dried chile puree on hand. Other "shortcuts" to consider are available at Mexican restaurants that provide "take out" foods. For example, you can buy puff taco shells, taco salad "bowls" (made from flour tor-tillas), and Pico de Gallo or salsa in pint or quart containers and prepare the rest at home. Cooking fajitas for a party is a lot easier if all you have to do is grill the meat. If a recipe calls for smoked or blackened chicken, duck, or some other item that requires special preparation, consider buying these items at a local restaurant to make your cooking job easier. A list of both fresh and pantry ingredients as well as the small equipment that is needed for the recipes in this book are listed on the following pages. Short definitions accompany unusual or unfamiliar items. See also the chile section for information on dried and fresh chiles. (pages 7–11)

Pantry Items

Chipotle chiles (canned in Adobo sauce)

Dried chiles (ancho, pasilla, cascabel, arbol, and chipotle)

Jalapeño chiles (canned or bottled)

Canned green chiles (diced and whole)

Picante sauce

Chicken and beef broth

Tomatoes (canned)

Tomatoes and green chiles (canned)

Pinto beans (canned, whole, refried, and dried)

Black beans (canned, whole, and dried)

Black bean dip (may be used for pureed black beans)

Capers

Tostadas (tortilla chips)

Dried corn husks

Safflower oil

Vegetable oil

Olive oil

Maple syrup

Honey

Barbecue sauce

Masa harina

Cornmeal (white, yellow, and blue)

Cumin

Chile powder

Leaf oregano

Garlic powder

Thyme

Cajun seasoning (a blend of cayenne pepper, salt, and spices)

Fajita seasoning

Soy sauce

Worcestershire sauce (gives a "smoky" flavor to grilled foods)

Achiote paste (usually found in Mexican markets)

Vinegars (white, rice wine, and balsamic)

Pecans

Pumpkin seeds (hulled, roasted)

Pine nuts

Fresh or Frozen Ingredients

Poblano chiles (will keep 3–4 days, refrigerated)

Jalapeño chiles (will keep 4–5 days, refrigerated)

Serrano chiles (will keep 4–5 days, refrigerated)

Tomatillos (small, green tomato-like fruit with a somewhat sticky husk—keeps about 1 week)

Fresh garlic

"Polander" garlic (minced garlic in small jars—must be refrigerated after opening)

Onions (red, white, and scallions)

Parsley (will keep up to 1 week when rinsed, stemmed, and completely dried. Store in paper-towel-lined plastic bags)

Cilantro (will keep up to 1 week when rinsed, stemmed, and completely dried. Store in paper-towel-lined plastic bags)

Jicama (a root vegetable that is crisp, white, low calorie, and tastes like a cross between an apple and fresh water chestnut)

Limes

Lemons

Orange juice (fresh or frozen)

Field greens

Cheeses
    Monterey Jack

Cheddar
Goat cheese
Cotija (or enchilada cheese)
Parmesan
Corn (fresh or frozen)
Tomatoes (preferably Roma)
Tortillas (corn and flour)
Sour cream
Buttermilk
Whipping cream (may be frozen
    and used thawed for most sauces)

Equipment

Blender
Food processor
Tortilla press
Ice cream scoops (several sizes)
Garlic press
Hand juicer
Plastic squirt bottles
Strainer
Parchment or microwave paper

FONDA SAN MIGUEL

Top Center: Almond Flan (pp. 220–221); *Right:* Coffee Toffee Pie (p. 224); *Bottom center:* Pescado Al Mojo de Ajo (p. 186); *Left:* Pollo Pibil (p. 162). Photo by Scott Moore.

HANDLING AND PREPARING HOT CHILE PEPPERS

Be sure to read the complete instructions before roasting the chiles.

Caution

When handling hot chile peppers, wear rubber gloves or generously oil your hands. Contact with the pepper oils will irritate the skin. Avoid rubbing your eyes because the oils will cause them to burn painfully.

Fresh Small Chiles (Jalapeño or Serrano)

Handle one at a time. With a sharp knife, cut away the stem; split the chile open. Remove the seeds with the tip of the knife. Pare away any large, fleshy veins. To make them somewhat less hot, soak prepared chiles in cold water for 1 hour. Or soak in a solution of 1 part each vinegar and water, a few tablespoons oil, and 1 teaspoon each sugar and salt. Refrigerate for a few days.

Canned Chiles

Rinse off the brine and seeds with cold water and pull away the stems before using the chiles.

To Roast Fresh Chiles and Sweet Red Peppers

Make a small slit in each chile and roast by one of the following methods.

Gas Stove. Spear the chiles with a long-handled fork and hold over the medium flame of a gas stove. Turn to be sure all the skin is charred. As long as the chiles are not left over the flame after blistered and charred, they will not burn. After they are completely blistered; rinse the skins off under cool water; then remove stems and seeds. The flesh will be bright green.

Electric Burner or Hot Plate. Put 3 or 4 chiles at a time on a wire rack. Spear as in gas stove method. Place over a burner set on medium to medium-high. Use tongs to turn the chiles so all sides are blistered and charred. Place chiles in heat-proof plastic freezer storage bags and freeze for 10 minutes or until ready to use (2 weeks to 6 months). If using immediately, rinse and then cut away stems, split open, and remove seeds.

Broiler. Preheat the broiler and set the chiles on a cookie sheet. Roast 4 to 6 inches away from heat source, turning to blister all sides. Transfer to plastic bags and freeze for 10 minutes or freeze as in preceding method.

Outdoor Grill. Roast the chiles when the smoke has subsided and all scent of any charcoal starter has evaporated. Use the hottest portion of the fire, moving the grate as close to the coals as possible. Turn the chiles to be sure all exposed surfaces are blistered and well charred. Remove and place immediately in heatproof plastic bags and then freeze for 10 minutes. (This stops the cooking process and makes the skin peel easily.) When peppers are roasted in this way, they have a wonderful flavor.

Small Propane Torch. This is a good method to prepare chiles for chiles rellenos or stuffed grilled chiles. Use a small propane torch, sometimes called a cook's torch. I am particularly fond of this method because the chiles stay firm and bright green. The torch easily reaches all the nooks and crannies, making the chiles easier to peel and more of the flesh usable. It is a superior method for chiles rellenos or the grilled chiles from La Fogata. Spear the stem portion with a long-handled fork. Open the fuel valve about ⅙ of a turn, allowing just enough propane to escape. Use a cigarette lighter and, when lit, increase the propane to make a 1½-to-2-inch flame. Torch all exposed areas of the chile until well charred. Let cool, then rinse under cold water to remove all the peel. (If freezing, leave skin intact.) This method also works well with both tomatoes and red bell peppers, leaving a firm product that will be less mushy. All peppers will sauté beautifully with this technique.

To Prepare Chiles Rellenos

Carefully make a slit down each chile and then, using scissors, cut away seeds and veins, taking care to leave the stem intact. Store in plastic bags until ready to use, no more than 12 hours.

Freezing

Always freeze chiles with charred skins intact, double-wrapped in freezerproof plastic bags.

▼▼▼

CHILES

New Mexico Green Chile

Many varieties with different names and degrees of hotness. Generally smaller than the California green chile, with a pointed tip, about 6–8 inches long, with a bright green color. Usually hot to hotter. Canned green chiles may be substituted (not jalapeños, which are smaller with a different flavor). These canned chiles are almost always milder; therefore, you may wish to add 1–2 jalapeño chiles to increase the hotness.

Poblano Chile

Large dark green chile, about the size of a green bell pepper, only narrower. Ranges from mild to hot, depending on the source and the season. No canned substitute.

California Anaheim

Large green chile, about 8 inches long, with a rounded tip and thick flesh. Generally mild, though when grown in the El Paso area, can be hotter. Bright green. Canned green chiles may be substituted.

Yellow Wax Chile

Small hot chile, about the size of a jalapeño. Use with restraint.

Jalapeño Chile

Small hot chile, ranging from 2–4 inches. Large ones generally less hot. Not usually roasted and peeled; rather, used fresh in relishes, sauces, or garnishes. Canned jalapeños are widely available and, though the color is less attractive, may be substituted.

Serrano Chile

Smaller than jalapeños, quite hot, though with a somewhat less harsh bite. Not usually roasted and peeled. Used for garnishes or salsas. Canned substitutes available.

Habañero Chile

Small, very hot bell-shaped chiles that are bright green, orange, and red. Used to flavor sauces or for a colorful garnish.

Chile Ancho

The dried poblano with a wrinkled skin. This is the chile from which chile con carne is made. Moderately mild to medium-hot. The chile powder made from this chile is a deep brick red. Gebhardt's Chile Powder is made from the chile ancho.

California Chile (Also Called Pasilla)

Smooth skin, brick red in color. The powder made from this chile is a brighter red than that from the chile ancho. Used for sauces, particularly with enchiladas. Some canned sauces are available.

New Mexico Chile (Also Called Ristra)

Usually a brighter red than the California chile and, if sun-dried, more translucent than other dried chiles. The powder made from these chiles is a bright red and always very hot. Some canned sauces are available made from this and the California chile, such as Las Palmas Red Chili Sauce.

Chile Chipotle

Dried chile (probably the jalapeño), canned in an orange-red, very hot sauce.

Chile Tepín and Chile Pequín

Small seedlike chiles originally used to preserve meats or to make beef jerky. Sometimes crushed and used in chile con carne or salsas.

Pasilla

Deep black, wrinkled-skin chile. Used in classic mole sauces along with chile ancho and other chiles. Not readily available.

Japone or Serrano Seco (Also Called Chile de Árbol)

Small, dried, very hot chile with a smooth skin. Used to flavor sauces, added whole rather than blended into a sauce like the larger dried chiles. Common also in Chinese cooking.

Cascabel Chile

Smooth skin, red-brown in color. This small chile is used in both raw and cooked salsas. Cascabels are often difficult to obtain; California or ancho chiles can be substituted.

Bottom left: Guacamole (p. 32); *middle:* Smoked Tomato Salsa (p. 30); *Right:* Chile con Queso (p. 62); *Top right:* Strawberry Margarita; *Top left:* Red Wine Sangria (p. 16)

BEVERAGES

GOLDEN MAMA
Cappy's

WHITE WINE SANGRÍA
Ninfa's

RED WINE SANGRÍA
Las Canarias

MAGIC SANGRÍA
Matt's Rancho Martinez

SOUTH AUSTIN MARGARITA
Matt's Rancho Martinez

"I'M NOT LYING THIS TIME" MARGARITA
Matt's Rancho Martinez

80-CALORIE MARGARITA
Matt's Rancho Martinez

GOLDEN MAMA

Cappy's version of a margarita is outstanding.

3	ounces Cuervo Gold
1½	ounces Grand Marnier
4–5	ounces sweet-and-sour mix
2–3	tablespoons fresh orange juice
1	cup, more or less, shaved ice
	salt
2	limes, sliced

In a blender or highball shaker, vigorously combine the ingredients.

Turn a collins or highball glass into a bowl of salt to lightly coat rim, then fill with Golden Mama.

Twist each lime slice to make a wheel. Garnish and serve.

Strawberry Margarita

Using a blender, blend above margarita with 4 frozen strawberries

▼▼▼

Ninfa's, Houston   Yield: About 5 servings

WHITE WINE SANGRÍA

This sangría is quite sweet. If you prefer a less sweet version, use the full bottle of wine.

½	cup fresh orange juice
½	cup pineapple juice
¼	cup water
4	tablespoons sugar

In a small saucepan, bring fruit juices, water, and sugar to a boil. Set aside to cool.

11	ounces white wine
2	ounces curaçao
1	ounce crème de banana
1	ounce brandy
¼	cup Sprite or 7-Up

Add the cooked syrup to the wine, liqueurs, brandy, and Sprite or 7-Up. Mix well.

1	lemon, thinly sliced and seeded
1	lime, thinly sliced and seeded
2	oranges, thinly sliced and seeded thin slices of fresh pineapple and maraschino cherries (optional)

Serve in 4–6 ounce glasses and garnish with fresh lemon, lime, and orange slices. If desired, add a few pineapple slices and cherries.

Storage, Freezing, and Advance Preparation

You may prepare this early in the day, but add the fruits just prior to serving.

▼▼

Las Canarias, *San Antonio*   Yield: About 16 servings

RED WINE SANGRÍA

This traditional sangría is a favorite beverage for Mexican specialties. The sweetness will vary according to the choice of red wine.

2 bottles red wine, preferably Burgundy, or a fruity wine 1 pint fresh orange juice juice of 6 lemons 1 pint ginger ale	In a large punch bowl, combine the wine, juices, and ginger ale.
2 lemons 4 limes 4 oranges	Thinly slice the lemons, limes, and oranges, and float in the Sangría prior to serving. Serve chilled over ice.

Storage, Freezing, and Advance Preparation

The Sangría may be prepared early in the day; however, add the fruit slices just prior to serving.

16

Matt's Rancho Martinez, *Dallas*   Yield: I

MAGIC SANGRÍA

Matt describes this as "pleasantly tart and great with spicy foods.' The rim of sugar and lime will give instant relief if you encounter an exceptionally hot chile!

I-10 ounce martini or sangría glass brown sugar Rose's lime juice	Whirl the brown sugar in a blender or food processor to remove any lumps. Place on a plate. Dip the rim of each glass first in Rose's lime juice, then in the brown sugar.

2 ounces red wine
I ounce peach or apricot
  brandy
2 ounces fresh orange juice
I lime wedge (¼ lime), juice only
  crushed ice
I slice fresh orange
	Fill the glass with red wine, brandy, orange juice, and juice from the lime wedge. Add crushed ice to the rim. Garnish with a fresh orange slice.

80-CALORIE MARGARITA

This low-calorie margarita is an invention of Matt Martinez.

I–10 ounce martini or margarita glass kosher salt Rose's lime juice	Put the salt on a small plate. Dip the rim of each glass first in Rose's lime juice, then in the salt.

¾ ounce fresh lime juice
I package artificial sweetener
I ounce Sauza Conmenoratizo
  Tequila
2 ounces water
  crushed ice
  fresh lime slice
	Fill the glass with lime juice, artificial sweetener, tequila and water.
	Stir to mix well. Add crushed ice to the rim and garnish with a fresh lime slice.

▼▼

Matt's Rancho Martinez, *Dallas*   Yield: 1

SOUTH AUSTIN MARGARITA

Matt's margaritas are made with crushed ice rather than blended in a margarita machine. If you prefer frozen margaritas, simply refrigerate all the ingredients and blend with the same amount of crushed ice. All Matt's margaritas use his fresh "Sweet and Sour." If you can get the small Mexican limes, the results are significantly better.

Fresh Sweet and Sour

1	cup fresh lime juice
1	cup sugar
4	cups water

Stir the lime juice and sugar together until all the sugar is dissolved. Add the water and stir to mix well. Set aside.

The Drink

1	10-ounce margarita glass
	kosher salt
	Rose's lime juice

Put the kosher salt on a shallow plate. Dip the glass rim first in Rose's lime juice, then in the salt.

1½	ounces tequila
½	fresh lime
	"splash" Contreau
	crushed ice
3	ounces fresh sweet and sour

Fill the glass with crushed ice. Stir together the tequila, juice from the half lime, Contreau, and fresh Sweet and Sour. Pour over the crushed ice.

1	lime wedge

Garnish with a lime wedge.

▼▼

Matt's Rancho Martinez, *Dallas*   Yield: 1

"I'M NOT LYING THIS TIME" MARGARITA

How many times have you heard someone claim "this is the best Margarita I've ever had . . ."? Matt Martinez claims this non-tequila margarita outsells every margarita at his restaurant.

Matt's Sweet and Sour

1	cup fresh lime juice
1	cup sugar
4	cups water

Stir the lime juice and sugar together until all the sugar is dissolved. Add the water and stir to mix well. Set aside.

The Drink

1	10-ounce highball or margarita glass
	package presweetened orange Kool-Aid
¼	teaspoon cayenne pepper
	Rose's lime juice

Combine the Kool-Aid and cayenne pepper and place in a shallow plate. Dip the rim of the glass in Rose's lime juice, then in the Kool-Aid mixture.

1	lime wedge (¼ lime)
1½	ounces Presidente brandy
	crushed ice
3	ounces Matt's Sweet and Sour

Squeeze the juice from the lime in the glass, leaving the wedge in the glass. Add brandy and then fill with crushed ice. Pour the Sweet and Sour over the ice, filling to the rim.

HUDSON'S ON THE BEND
Hot and Crunchy Trout with Ancho Mayonnaise (p. 155); Mango Salsa (p. 184); and Corn Pudding (p. 118)

Relishes, Salsas, and Fillings

Ninfa's Red Sauce
Ninfa's

Green Chile Salsa
La Hacienda

Pico de Gallo
Mariano's

Ernesto's Hot Sauce
Ernesto's

Chile and Cilantro Pesto
Blue Mesa

Black Bean Relish
Boudro's

Corn and Black Bean Relish
Cappy's

Roasted Tomato Salsa
Author's Contribution

Smoked Tomato Salsa
Matt's Ranchero Martinez

Salsa
Author's Contribution

Guacamole
Author's Contribution

Roasted Garlic and White Bean Dip
Mark Gonzales

Enchilada Sauce
Blue Mesa

Chipotle Cream Sauce
Blue Mesa

Ranchera Sauce
Mesa

Red Bell Pepper Sauce
Blue Mesa

Sour Cream Sauce
Casa Rosa

Chile Cascabel Sauce
Casa Rosa

Black Bean Sauce
Cappy's

Tomatillo Sauce
Matt's Rancho Martinez

Salsa Verde de Tomatillo
Blue Mesa

Chile Arbol Sauce
Kokopelli

▼▼

Ninfa's, *Houston*   Yield: 2 cups

NINFA'S RED SALSA

If good ripe, fresh tomatoes are not available, you may want to add some tomato sauce or the juice from canned Italian-style tomatoes when sautéing the salsa. Or substitute canned Italian-style tomatoes. It is not necessary to peel the tomatoes; however, this is a matter of personal preference.

1–2	chiles de árboles or 1–2 slender, hot, dried red peppers, such as japones

Place the dried chiles on a cookie sheet and toast in a 325-degree oven for about 3 to 4 minutes. Stem and seed and set aside.

4	medium-size tomatoes, halved
3	cloves garlic
4	cilantro sprigs
1	teaspoon salt
1–2	jalapeño chiles (optional)

In a medium-size skillet, simmer the tomatoes and garlic, in just enough water to prevent scorching, until softened—about 20 minutes. Transfer to a blender and puree along with the cilantro, salt, toasted chiles, and if desired, jalapeños, for 1 to 2 minutes.

1–2	tablespoons oil
½	cup tomato sauce (optional)

Sauté the pureed salsa in a skillet with hot oil for 1 to 2 minutes. If the salsa is pale, you may wish to add some tomato sauce to deepen the color.

Storage, Freezing, and Advance Preparation

The salsa may be made in advance and either refrigerated or frozen.

▼▼

La Hacienda, *San Antonio*   Yield: About 6½ cups

Green Chile Salsa

This New Mexico specialty may be served hot or cold, but either way it is fast becoming a Texas crowd pleaser. It is often served with chips, much as a Texas salsa, and in this way it disappears rapidly. It is best made in this quantity.

1	medium-size onion, chopped
1	tablespoon butter

In a large skillet, sauté the onion in butter until soft and translucent.

½	pound ground beef or pork
1	clove garlic, minced
1½	teaspoons salt or to taste
½	teaspoon ground cumin

Add the ground meat, garlic, and seasonings and sauté until the beef is cooked.

2	pounds mild to hot California Anaheim or New Mexico green chiles, roasted and peeled, chopped, or canned mild green chiles, rinsed, or New Mexico frozen green chiles
1	green tomato, minced
3	tomatillos, finely chopped
1–2	tablespoons granulated sugar, depending on the type of chiles used
½	cup, more or less, chicken stock

Add the chiles, tomato, tomatillos, sugar, and stock and simmer 15 to 20 minutes. Add more stock as necessary to prevent the meat or chiles from sticking. Taste and adjust seasonings. Canned chiles may require more salt or sugar.

Serve hot or cold.

Variation

If you add extra stock and cook 10 to 15 minutes more, this may be used as a sauce for enchiladas or chimichangas or as a stew. This will require more salt or sugar.

Author's Note

A pound of chiles is equal to about 10 whole chiles. If you are using the 3-ounce cans of chiles, it takes about 8 cans to make 2 pounds, as called for above. Do not substitute jalapeños.

Storage, Freezing, and Advance Preparation

The sauce may be made 2 to 3 days in advance; it freezes quite well.

Yield: 2–2½ cups

PICO DE GALLO

This chopped relish has become so popular for a variety of dishes that to choose the best is nearly impossible. Recipes are all very much the same—some use jalapeños, some serranos. The key is to select the best possible tomatoes and the freshest cilantro.

½   cup onions, diced

1–2   tablespoons cilantro, chopped

1–3   jalapeño chiles, stemmed, seeded, and chopped

2   cups (2–3 medium-size) tomatoes, peeled and diced

½   teaspoon salt or to taste squeeze of fresh lime juice

Combine the onions, cilantro, and jalapeños in a glass bowl.

Add the tomatoes and mix together thoroughly. Add salt and fresh lime juice to taste.

Serve as a relish or salsa for other dishes or as a dip with tostados.

Storage, Freezing, and Advance Preparation

This relish keeps well, refrigerated, for 1–2 days.

Variation

This basic salsa can be a base for many variations. Add diced mango, cooked black beans, grilled corn kernels, or diced papaya.

▼▼▼

Ernesto's, *San Antonio*   Yield: 3 cups

ERNESTO'S HOT SAUCE

This recipe is Ernesto's specialty and one of his most successful trade secrets. It is delicious served with tostados, chilled shrimp, grilled beef, or seafood appetizers.

15–16	(about 1 pound) tomatillos, halved
1–2	teaspoons sugar
5	serrano chiles, stemmed and seeded
1	clove garlic, finely minced
2	tablespoons white vinegar
¾	cup cooking oil, heated
½	teaspoon salt or to taste

In a medium-size saucepan, bring the tomatillos, sugar, serranos, garlic, and vinegar to a boil. Simmer 8 to 10 minutes.

Transfer the cooked tomatillo mixture to a blender. Process until smooth and light in consistency—about 2 minutes. Then, while the machine is still running, pour the oil through the feed tube. When all the oil has been added, adjust salt to taste.

Serve the sauce either hot or cold.

Storage, Freezing, and Advance Preparation

The sauce loses its texture with freezing but keeps well for 2 weeks refrigerated. Reblend, if necessary, to restore texture.

Author's Note

After cooking, blend the sauce with ½–¾ cups parsley or cilantro sprigs to achieve a brighter green color.

▼▼▼

Blue Mesa, *Dallas*   Yield: 1 cup

CHILE AND CILANTRO PESTO

The popularity of cilantro and chile pestos in Mexican restaurants has spread like mesquite wildfire. Some have pine nuts, some pumpkin seeds; there are infinite versions. This is the one Blue Mesa uses in many of their dishes.

1	poblano chile, roasted, peeled and chopped
4	cups fresh cilantro (loosely packed), well rinsed
3	cloves garlic
3	ounces Parmesan cheese, grated
¼	cup pine nuts
½–¾	cups light olive oil
	salt and pepper to taste
	squeeze of fresh lemon juice

Using a food processor fitted with the metal blade, process the chile, cilantro, and garlic until finely minced.

Add the Parmesan cheese and pine nuts and process to combine. Add the oil last, using enough to make a moist, spreadable consistency. Season to taste with salt, pepper, and fresh lemon juice.

Variation

Use pumpkin seeds in place of pine nuts. Add about 1 cup parsley along with the cilantro to make a brighter green color.

Storage, Freezing and Advance Preparation

The pesto keeps for 3–4 days or freezes well. Float 1–2 tablespoons oil on top of the pesto and store covered.

▼▼

Boudro's, *San Antonio*   Yield: 4 cups

BLACK BEAN RELISH

This relish is more like an accompaniment and is served with the Pork Tenderloin at Boudro's. Be sure the beans are whole and unbroken, but tender.

½   pound black beans, rinsed
½   gallon (more or less) water
3–4 chicken bouillon cubes
     (see note)
     salt and pepper

Rinse the beans, removing any stones. Bring the beans, water, and chicken bouillon cubes to a boil in a large saucepan. Reduce the heat and simmer until the beans are tender but still whole, 1½ to 2 hours. Drain and rinse with cold water to stop the cooking process. Season the beans with salt and pepper.

½   cup diced jicama
½   cup fresh corn kernels,
     blanched
¼   cup balsamic vinegar
¼   cup light olive oil
2   tablespoons maple syrup
1   tablespoon white wine vinegar
2   shallots, minced
¼   cup chopped cilantro
     pinch cumin
     salt and pepper to taste

Combine the jicama, corn, vinegars, oil, maple syrup, shallots, cilantro, and cumin in a glass bowl. Season to taste with salt and pepper.

½   red bell pepper, roasted and
     peeled

Dice the bell pepper into ¼-inch dice. Stir peppers and black beans carefully into the relish, to prevent breaking the beans.

NOTE: Boudro's uses a rich, flavorful chicken stock to cook the beans. You may want to add several strips of bacon, onion, and garlic to the cooking water. Discard vegetables when rinsing the beans.

Cappy's, *San Antonio*   Yield: 2 cups

CORN AND BLACK BEAN RELISH

You'll find many uses for this delicious, colorful relish. Cappy uses it in his Quesadillas but try it on fried catfish, with grilled chicken, or to accompany enchiladas. Be sure only to use whole, unbruised black beans, and rinse them well.

¼	cup light olive oil
2	tablespoons fresh lime juice
2	serrano chiles, seeded and minced
1	cup frozen corn kernels or fresh corn, blanched
1	cup whole, cooked black beans, rinsed
¼	cup minced red onion
1	teaspoon sea salt
½	teaspoon pepper

Whisk together the olive oil and lime juice in a mixing bowl. Add the remaining ingredients and mix gently, so not to bruise the beans.

Refrigerate until ready to use.

NOTE: See page 119 for cooking procedure for beans.

▼▼

Author's Contribution   Yield: 2 cups

ROASTED TOMATO SALSA

This simple but flavorful salsa is best when made with vine-ripened or home-grown tomatoes. Roma or cherry tomatoes will usually produce the best flavor.

	light olive oil
8	Roma tomatoes, cores intact, or
2	boxes medium-large cherry tomatoes
4–6	serrano chiles
	salt and pepper to taste
1–2	tablespoons fresh cilantro (optional)

Lightly oil both the tomatoes and chiles and place them on a preheated charcoal grill or indoor grill on the highest heat.

Turn the tomatoes and chiles to grill and char all sides. Cover the grill and continue to cook until the tomatoes are soft, about 10–12 minutes for Roma tomatoes, 5 minutes for cherry tomatoes. If the chiles get too black, move them to a cooler portion of the grill or reduce the heat. Transfer the tomatoes and stemmed chiles to a food processor or blender and blend with on/offs until very finely chopped and the skin disappears.

Season the salsa to taste with salt and pepper. Stir in cilantro, if desired.

▼▼▼

Matt's Rancho Martinez, *Dallas*   Yield: 4 servings

SMOKED TOMATO SALSA

Mexican chefs have been influenced by the "smoking trend" in the Southwest. Smoking is no longer reserved for meat alone. If you do not have a smoker, you may use any barbecue grill and soaked wood chips, or simply grill the tomatoes, onion, and garlic.

Preparing the Grill

Build a hot fire, or set the temperature of a gas grill to high. While the fire is heating, soak about 2 cups of wood chips in water. Drain the water and place the chips on either side of the grill. Spread out the coals and add the wood chips around them. If using a gas grill, put the wood chips on foil and place on the rack. Scatter a few over the lava rocks. The gas grill will have less "smoke" flavor.

3	whole, medium-size tomatoes
1	clove garlic
½	sweet white onion
6	serrano chiles or 3 jalapeño chiles

Put the tomatoes, garlic, onion, and chiles on the grill rack. Spear the garlic and chiles with a toothpick so they don't fall through the grids.

Cover and smoke about 45 minutes, or until vegetables are soft. Check the grill occasionally. If the wood chips burn, add additional soaked chips. The vegetables will only take about 20–30 minutes on a gas grill, as the temperature will be hotter. You will need to remove the garlic and chiles after 8–10 minutes.

2	tablespoons vegetable oil
1	teaspoon vinegar
	salt to taste
2	teaspoons cornstarch
1	tablespoon water

Put the tomatoes, stemmed chiles, garlic, and onion in a food processor fitted with the metal blade and use the pulse with on/offs to chop coarsely. (Do not use a blender). Add oil and vinegar and season to taste with salt. If the salsa is too liquid, dissolve the cornstarch in water and drizzle into the salsa over medium heat, stirring constantly for 2–3 minutes.

▼▼

SALSA

Each restaurant has its own signature red sauce. This is a general recipe that uses canned tomatoes—a good substitute when fresh tomatoes are out of season.

Salsa

2	cloves garlic, peeled
4	jalapeño chiles, stemmed (not seeded)
1	large white or yellow onion, peeled and cut into 8 pieces
2	16-ounce cans chopped or plum tomatoes, including juices
1	teaspoon salt
½–⅓	cup cilantro leaves
1	tablespoon fresh lime juice
½–1	teaspoon sugar

Using a food processor fitted with the metal blade, drop the garlic cloves through the feed tube and process to mince.

Add chiles and process until finely chopped. Add onion pieces, tomatoes, salt, and cilantro and process until pureed.

Season with fresh lime juice and sugar.

Variation

Some restaurants sweat the onion in a small amount of oil and add this to the finished salsa instead of adding the raw onion with the tomatoes. Others add both sautéed onion and fresh chopped tomatoes to the finished salsa.

▼▼

Author's Contribution   Yield: 1½–2 cups

GUACAMOLE

Some chefs use lime, some lemon, some add a pinch of chile powder, others add tomatoes and onions—but all agree guacamole is best when made just before serving and mashed by hand. For best results, buy avocados while still firm and let them ripen at home for several days. Guacamole needs a lot of salt, so if it seems bland you may need more salt.

2	ripe avocados, peeled and pitted
2	cloves fresh garlic, minced
1	tablespoon fresh lemon juice
1	tablespoon finely minced green chiles
1	tablespoon chopped sweet onion
	sea salt to taste
1–2	tablespoons fresh minced cilantro (optional)
1	Roma tomato, diced (optional)
1	tomatillo, pureed (optional)

In a wooden bowl, mash together the avocado, garlic, lemon juice, and green chiles. Add sweet onion and salt and pepper to taste. If using, stir in fresh cilantro and tomato.

Add 1 tomatillo, pureed, to help preserve the fresh, green color. Reduce the lemon juice, as tomatillos add a lemon flavor.

Mark Gonzales, Chef, *Dallas*   Yield: 2 cups

ROASTED GARLIC AND WHITE BEAN DIP

Mark uses this bean puree on his Fish Tacos (p. 144). You could make this recipe with pinto or black beans. You can also serve this dip warm, topped with Pico de Gallo, on tortilla chips. A two-color dip, one made with white beans, the other with black beans, makes a colorful appetizer.

It you prefer a spicier dip, increase the jalapeño chiles, or use 1–2 chipotle chiles when blending the beans.

14	large cloves garlic, skin on
½	pound white beans, soaked overnight
8	cups chicken stock
1	large onion, diced
1	jalapeño chile, stemmed and halved
2	tablespoons olive oil
1	tablespoon shallot, minced
1	tablespoon ground sea salt
1	teaspoon ground cumin
2	teaspoons fresh cracked black pepper
2	tablespoons chopped cilantro
2	tablespoons fresh lemon juice
2–3	tablespoons light olive oil

Roast the garlic in a 250° oven for 35–45 minutes or until very soft. Cool, peel, and set aside.

Cook the beans with the onion and jalapeño in simmering chicken stock for 1½–2 hours or until very soft. Drain and reserve the broth.

In a small saucepan over medium heat, saute the shallots in hot oil until softened. Set aside.

Transfer the garlic, beans, onion, jalapeño and sauteed shallots to a food processor fitted with the metal blade. Add seasonings, lemon juice, and olive oil. Process to a smooth consistency. Add additional reserved broth as needed to make a soft consistency.

Top the bean dip with Pico de Gallo and serve with tortilla chips.

Blue Mesa, *Dallas*   Yield: 4 cups

ENCHILADA SAUCE

This is an excellent basic recipe for enchilada sauce made with ancho chiles. Blue Mesa uses it on their Adobe Pie, as well as for enchiladas. The Chipotle Cream Sauce that follows is also used on Adobe Pie, but you will love it on all enchiladas.

2	tablespoons shortening or corn oil
½	cup sliced onions
2	cloves minced garlic
½	cup canned, diced tomatoes, including juices
1	cup Ancho Chile Puree (p. 156)
1	tablespoon pureed chipotle chiles
1½	cups chicken broth
¼	teaspoon leaf oregano
¼	teaspoon cumin
1	bay leaf
1	tablespoon sugar
1	tablespoon cider vinegar

In a medium skillet, heat the shortening or corn oil over medium heat and saute the onions and garlic until lightly browned. Cool slightly and then transfer to a blender jar. Add canned tomatoes and blend smooth. Pour back into a saucepan and add the chile puree, and chipotle chiles. Stir in chicken broth and seasonings and simmer 4–5 minutes.

2	tablespoons margarine
1½	tablespoons flour

Melt the margarine in a small skillet and stir in the flour to make a roux. Cook until light brown, and whisk into the simmering sauce. Simmer, stirring often, for about 8–10 minutes. Strain through a coarse strainer. Season to taste with salt and pepper.

CHIPOTLE CREAM SAUCE

Chipotle Puree

1 can chipotle chiles in adobe	Put the chipotle chiles in a blender jar and blend on high speed until pureed. Set aside 2 tablespoons for the sauce and refrigerate the rest for another use.
1 ounce dry sherry ½ cup whipping cream 2 tablespoons chipotle puree salt to taste	Bring the sherry to a boil in a saucepan and boil for 2–3 minutes. Add the cream, chipotle puree, and salt and bring to a simmer, stirring often.
1¾ cups Enchilada Sauce (p. 34)	Add the Enchilada Sauce and stir to combine. Heat to a simmer and cook 2–3 minutes, or until hot. Adjust salt and pepper to taste.

▼▼

Mesa, *Houston*   Yield: 6 cups

RANCHERA SAUCE

Mesa uses this sauce as a base for many of their sauces. It has a distinct tomato flavor, well seasoned with chiles and herbs. Combined with corn puree and cream, it makes a pasta sauce, or use it as is with any of your favorite enchilada or egg dishes.

1	piece bacon, finely minced
1	large onion, minced
2	cloves garlic, minced
¼	cup chile powder
1½	14-½ ounce cans diced tomatoes
2	cups tomato juice
1	teaspoon ground cumin
2	chicken bouillon cubes
	salt and pepper to taste

Sauté the bacon in a large saucepan until browned. Add the onion and garlic and cook until translucent. Stir in the chile powder and immediately add the tomatoes, tomato juice, oregano, cumin, and bouillon cubes. Reduce the heat and simmer the sauce for 20–25 minutes, stirring occasionally, until ingredients are combined, thickened, and flavorful. Adjust salt and pepper to taste.

NOTE: This is a chunky sauce and quite mild. If you prefer a spicier sauce, add 1 poblano chile, roasted, peeled and diced or 2 jalapeño chiles, minced.

Blue Mesa, *Dallas*   Yield: 1½–2 cups

RED BELL PEPPER SAUCE

Blue Mesa serves this sauce with their Crab and Shrimp Cakes. It is equally good with grilled seafood and fresh fish or with Wild Mushroom Enchiladas on p. 131.

3   red bell peppers, roasted and
        peeled (about 1 cup pureed)

Put the red bell peppers in a blender and blend with on/offs to chop, then blend until smooth. Add a small amount of white wine, if necessary, to aid blending.

¾   cup white wine
¼   cup white vinegar
⅓   cup diced onions
2   cloves garlic, minced
⅛   teaspoon salt
⅛   teaspoon pepper
½   cup heavy cream
¼   pound butter, in pieces

Bring the wine, vinegar, onions, and garlic to a boil in a saucepan. Simmer over medium heat until liquid is reduced by about half the original volume. Add salt, pepper, and cream and continue to boil to reduce for 4–5 minutes. Reduce the heat to low, and stir in the bell pepper puree. Slowly add the butter pieces, stirring constantly, until all the butter is incorporated.

Adjust seasonings to taste and strain through a fine strainer. Keep warm in a double boiler, over hot water, until ready to use.

▼▼▼

Casa Rosa   Yield: 2 cups

SOUR CREAM SAUCE

Casa Rosa offers a choice of sauces for all their enchiladas. This sauce is a good match for their Wild Mushroom Enchiladas or Shrimp Enchiladas.

1	cup water	Bring water, lemon juice, and bouillon cubes to a boil. Reduce heat to a simmer.
1	teaspoon lemon juice	
2	chicken bouillon cubes	

3   tablespoons all purpose flour
3   tablespoons butter, melted

Mix together the flour and butter to make a smooth paste. Slowly add the mixture to the simmering liquid, stirring constantly. Cook over medium-low heat until thickened and smooth, about 3–4 minutes.

1½   cups sour cream
        salt and pepper to taste

Stir in the sour cream over low heat. Do not boil or the sauce will break. Season to taste with salt and pepper.

▼▼

Casa Rosa, *Dallas*   Yield: 3 cups

CHILE CASCABEL SAUCE

This sauce is served on the Wild Mushroom Enchilada at Casa Rosa, but is delicious on any of your favorite enchiladas. Cascabel chiles are found in most Texas supermarkets or specialty stores that carry Mexican ingredients.

Cascabel Puree

½	pound dried cascabel chiles, stemmed and seeded
I	pound fresh tomatoes, cleaned and quartered
4	cups chicken broth, including fat

Bring the chiles to a boil in enough water to cover. Simmer until softened, about 10 minutes. Strain and discard water. Blend the chiles with tomatoes and about 4 cups chicken broth. Strain again. Bring to a boil and cook 6–8 minutes, or until the consistency of a thick tomato sauce. Season with salt. Set aside 1 cup for the sauce and refrigerate the rest for another use.

Tomato-Jalapeño Puree

2	fresh jalapeño chiles
7	fresh tomatoes

Put the jalapeño chiles and tomatoes on a grill and grill on all sides until charred. Remove stems and place tomatoes and chiles in a blender jar. Blend until smooth. Set aside.

2	tablespoons chopped bacon
I	cup diced onions
2	tablespoons flour

In a medium skillet, sauté the bacon for about a minute. Add onion and cook until lightly browned. Stir in the flour and cook about 1 minute.

1½	cups tomato-jalapeño puree
I	cup cascabel puree
½	cup beef broth
I	teaspoon cumin
½	teaspoon garlic powder
I	teaspoon salt
I	bay leaf, crushed

Add 1½ cups of the Tomato Puree, 1 cup Cascabel Pureé, and all the seasonings, stirring constantly until smooth and thickened.

½	cup buttermilk

Reduce the heat and slowly stir in the buttermilk. DO NOT BOIL. Strain the sauce and adjust seasonings to taste.

BLACK BEAN SAUCE

Cappy serves this sauce on his Santa Fe Chicken, a popular menu item at Cappy's. Canned beans, including their liquid, may be used in place of the lengthy task of soaking and cooking beans. It is surprisingly low in fat.

1	clove minced garlic
2	tablespoons chopped cilantro
2	tablespoons chopped parsley
½	stalk celery, chopped
¼	cup chopped onion
⅛	cup picante sauce
1½	cups chicken broth
1½	cups cooked black beans
	salt and pepper to taste

Put all the ingredients in a large saucepan and bring to a boil. Reduce the heat and simmer, uncovered, for 15–20 minutes.

In several batches, puree the beans and liquid in a blender. Cool and refrigerate until ready to use.

Thin the sauce with chicken broth, if necessary, when reheating. Adjust seasonings with salt and pepper as needed.

Note: If using canned black beans, use 1 16-ounce can. Drain to separate liquid from the beans and add enough chicken broth to the liquid to make 1½ cups total. Proceed as directed.

▼▼

Matt's Rancho Martinez, *Dallas*   Yield: 4 cups

TOMATILLO SAUCE

This sauce is one of the most requested recipes at Rancho Martinez. It is used traditionally for chicken enchiladas, but Matt uses it on fresh grilled catfish. It is equally good on grilled salmon.

| ½ | pound fresh tomatillos | Remove husks from tomatillos and quarter. Using a food processor fitted with the metal blade, pulse to finely mince tomatillos. |

2	tablespoons vegetable oil
½	cup chopped onions
½	teaspoon sugar
1	teaspoon salt
1	fresh jalapeño, stemmed and diced
¼	cup chopped cilantro
1½	cups chopped spinach
3	cups chicken broth

In a large saucepan, heat the vegetable oil over medium heat. Add the onions and sauté until translucent, 2–3 minutes. Add tomatillos, sugar, salt, jalapeño, cilantro, spinach, and chicken broth. Simmer on low heat for about 20 minutes.

| 2 | teaspoons cornstarch |

Dissolve the cornstarch in about 1 tablespoon water and slowly drizzle into the sauce to thicken. Simmer, stirring constantly, for 1–2 minutes. Adjust salt and pepper to taste.

Blue Mesa, *Dallas*   Yield: 3½ cups

SALSA VERDE DE TOMATILLO

This low-fat Tomatillo Sauce is used on Chicken and Mushroom Enchiladas for a light lunch entrée at Blue Mesa, and it has become one of their most popular menu items.

1	pound fresh tomatillos, peeled, cleaned and quartered
1½	cups water
2	serrano chiles, stemmed and chopped
2	tablespoons chopped Romaine lettuce
½	bunch fresh cilantro, chopped
4	green onions, green and white part, chopped
3	chicken bouillon cubes
1	poblano chile, roasted, peeled, and diced
1	clove garlic, peeled
¼	cup minced parsley
2	teaspoons cornstarch
¼	cup water
	salt to taste

Put all the ingredients, except the parsley, in a large saucepan and bring to a boil. Reduce the heat to medium and simmer, uncovered, until the tomatillos are tender, about 10–12 minutes. Transfer the mixture to a food processor or blender jar, add the parsley, and blend until smooth. It will be necessary to do this in several batches.

Return the sauce to the same saucepan over medium heat. Combine the cornstarch and water and stir to dissolve. Slowly add the cornstarch to the sauce, stirring constantly. Cook for 4–5 minutes, or until thickened. Season to taste with salt.

Kokopelli, *Dallas* Yield: 2½ cups

CHILE ÁRBOL SAUCE

Árbol chiles are small, slender red chiles that are commonly called "tree chiles." They are very hot, but are tamed by the tomatillos in this sauce. They make a delicious dipping sauce you will use on many of your favorite dishes or simply as a dip with tostadas.

2	árbol chiles, stemmed
1	ancho chile, stemmed
2	ounces olive oil
¼	small white onion, diced
1	serrano chile, minced
5	tomatillos, peeled and diced
2	cloves garlic, minced

Cut the chiles in several places.

Heat the olive oil in a saucepan over medium heat. Add the árbol and ancho chiles and cook over medium-low heat for 2–3 minutes or until soft. Add onion, serrano, tomatillos, and garlic and cook on low heat until the vegetables are medium-brown in color.

½	cup apple cider vinegar
10–12	cilantro stems
3½	cups water
1	teaspoon chile powder
1	teaspoon cumin

Add vinegar and cilantro stems and boil to reduce liquid by half. Add the water and simmer until the chiles are soft, about 10 minutes. Stir in cumin and chile powder. Cook an additional 5 minutes. Remove from heat and cool.

salt to taste

Blend the mixture until very smooth. Strain to remove seeds and chile skins. Season to taste with salt.

HUDSON'S ON THE BEND
Tortilla Crusted Quail on Mixed Greens (p. 184)

BRUNCH DISHES

YUCATAN QUICHE
Bennie Ferrell Catering

EGGS MAXIMILIAN
Cappy's

TEX-MEX CAPIROTADA
Mariano's

NEW MEXICAN ENCHILADAS
La Hacienda

CHILE QUICHE
Bennie Ferrell Catering

HUEVOS RANCHEROS
Author's Contribution

GAZPACHO OMELET
Bennie Ferrell Catering

FRUIT QUESADILLAS
Casa Rosa

Bennie Ferrell Catering, *Houston*

Yield: 6 servings

YUCATÁN QUICHE

The Crust

| ¾–1 | cup safflower oil |
| 7–8 | corn tortillas |

In a medium-size skillet, heat the safflower oil. Dip each tortilla briefly to soften and seal and then press between paper towels.

Spray a 9-inch pie pan with a nonstick vegetable coating and then line with the prepared tortillas, overlapping them, extending about ½ inch over the pan edge.

The Filling

2	eggs
2	cups half-and-half or cream
½	teaspoon salt
2	cups (about 8 ounces) shredded Monterey Jack cheese
1	cup refried beans
½	pound sausage, cooked and drained
2	tablespoons mild green chiles, diced

In a small bowl, combine the eggs, half-and-half or cream, and salt. Set aside.

Sprinkle half the cheese over the tortillas, followed by the beans, sausage, chiles, and then the egg mixture. Evenly distribute the remaining cheese over the top. Bake in a preheated 350° oven for 30 minutes or until firm.

Presentation

1	avocado, diced
1	tomato, sliced
	snipped cilantro leaves

Garnish the baked quiche with avocado and tomato slices. Place cilantro leaves over the top. Serve warm.

Storage, Freezing, and Advance Preparation

This is as good at room temperature as it is hot, but it does not freeze very well.

EGGS MAXIMILIAN

Cappy's flavorful sauce is prepared without butter or oil, which makes it a low-calorie sauce, perfect for eggs, chicken, fish, or grilled meats. To save preparation time, you may use crisp tortilla shells or toasted English muffins in place of masa cups. If fresh masa is not easy to obtain, use masa harina, adding 1 teaspoon sugar and 1 tablespoon cornmeal to the package directions.

The Ranchero Sauce

1	2½-pound can whole tomatoes
1	onion, chopped
1	bell pepper, seeded and chopped
4	cloves garlic, minced
3	tomatoes, chopped
3–4	serrano chiles, finely minced
	snipped cilantro
1	cup water
4	ounces tomato paste
1½	teaspoons salt or to taste
½	teaspoon black pepper
½	teaspoon leaf oregano
½	teaspoon ground cumin

Drain all the juice from the canned tomatoes into a large saucepan. Roughly chop the tomatoes, combine with all the other vegetables, and bring to a boil.

Add water, tomato paste, and seasonings and return to a boil. Reduce heat and simmer for 20 minutes.

The Poached Eggs

1	poached egg per serving
	butter

Poach the eggs and hold them at room temperature, brushed with butter, while preparing the masa cups.

Cappy's

The Fresh Masa

fresh corn masa (about 1 ounce
per mold)
peanut oil for frying

Spray 3-inch fluted tin molds with a nonstick vegetable coating. Pinch off a ball of masa and then press into molds. Deep-fry, using tongs, in oil heated to 375°. The molds will sink to the bottom and, as the masa cooks, it will separate from the molds and float. Turn to fry both sides. Take care not to overcook or the masa cups may become tough. Drain on paper towels.

NOTE: To make masa from masa harina, combine 1 cup dry masa with 1 cup water and 1 tablespoon melted margarine.

Assembly and Presentation

grated cheddar cheese
chopped fresh parsley

Use one poached egg per masa cup. Ladle sauce over each egg. Top with cheddar cheese and place 4 inches under the broiling element, just long enough to melt the cheese.

Garnish with chopped parsley. Serve with fresh sliced fruit and seasonal berries.

Storage, Freezing, and Advance Preparation

The sauce may be made a day ahead or several weeks ahead and frozen. The eggs may be poached the night before (if preparing for a large crowd), removed from the poaching liquid when slightly undercooked, and then held in ice-cold water overnight. Reheat by submerging in hot water about 1 minute and 20 seconds. The masa shells are best when made just prior to serving.

▼▼

Mariano's, *Dallas*   Yield: 12–14 servings

TEX-MEX CAPIROTADA

This is a most unusual combination as well as technique for this Tex-Mex bread pudding. When I first assembled it, it smelled like banana cream pie . . . a bit rich for dessert, unless served in very small portions. It makes an excellent brunch buffet item, served with whipped cream.

The Pudding Mixture

12	slices stale bread, preferably French or whole wheat
8–10	ounces grated Monterey Jack or cubed cream cheese
¾	cup pitted prunes, plumped in hot water and diced
¾	cup seedless white raisins or dates, diced
2	large bananas, sliced, or coarsely chopped apples
1	cup sliced almonds

Toast the bread and allow to cool. Using a well-buttered baking dish, 12 by 9 by 2 inches, make a layer of bread, using about half the bread. Top with half the cheese and fruits and all the bananas or apples. Add another bread layer, then the remaining cheese, fruits, and the nuts. Set aside.

The Syrup

2	cups water
1½	cups brown sugar, packed
½	teaspoon cinnamon

In a medium-size saucepan, boil the water, sugar, and cinnamon together for 5 minutes. Pour over the pudding mixture.

Mariano's

The Egg Mixture and Topping

2	cups water
1	cup granulated sugar
4	eggs, separated
4	tablespoons flour

In the same saucepan, boil the water and sugar for 5 minutes. Remove 1 cup and beat with egg yolks and flour, then add this egg mixture to the remaining syrup and cook over medium heat, stirring constantly, for 5 minutes or until thick. Pour this custard over the bread and fruits.

Cover and let stand several hours at room temperature, or refrigerate overnight.

The Meringue

	reserved egg whites
2	tablespoons granulated sugar

When ready to bake the pudding, beat the egg whites until very stiff, beating in the sugar at the last. Spread atop the pudding and then bake at 350° for about 40 minutes, or until the meringue is well browned and the pudding is set.

Presentation

sweetened whipped cream
or ice cream

Serve small portions with a dollop of ice cream or whipped cream.

Storage, Freezing, and Advance Preparation

The basic dessert, excluding the topping, may be prepared 24 hours in advance or overnight. Because of the sweet syrups, the bananas will not turn brown any faster than they would during ordinary baking. The topping should be added just prior to baking. The pudding may be served either hot or cold; it will reheat easily without changing consistency, either in a microwave oven or in a hot 400° oven, covered with foil.

▼▼▼

La Hacienda, *San Antonio*   Yield: 4 servings

NEW MEXICAN ENCHILADAS

This dish is one of my favorites for brunch, lunch, or dinner. The enchiladas are stacked like pancakes and topped with an egg. Because the New Mexico sun-dried red chile pod is difficult to obtain, I have given a method which uses a canned enchilada sauce. Though not traditional, fresh tomatoes tame the sauce, which may be prepared in advance.

1	small onion, chopped
1½	cups Monterey Jack cheese, grated
1½	cups cheddar cheese, grated
½	small onion, chopped (optional)
1–2	tablespoons vegetable oil
1	1-pound can tomatoes, crushed
2	tomatoes, peeled and chopped
1–1½	cups chicken stock
1½	teaspoons salt
½	teaspoon garlic powder
½	teaspoon ground cumin
1	teaspoon leaf oregano
1–1½	cups canned enchilada sauce
4–5	tablespoons tomato paste, if needed
	vegetable oil
1	dozen corn tortillas

Using a strainer, rinse the onion with cold water to remove all bitterness. Toss the cheese and onion together. Set aside.

Sauté the onion, if using, in 1–2 tablespoons hot oil for 10 to 12 minutes. Add the drained canned tomatoes and the fresh tomatoes and transfer to a blender or a food processor to puree. Return the puree to a medium-size saucepan and stir in the chicken stock, seasonings, and the enchilada sauce. Cook 30 minutes, stirring occasionally. As the sauce simmers and reduces, it will thicken. If necessary, stir in tomato paste to thicken further.

In a medium-size skillet, heat oil to about 300°. Pass tortillas into hot oil for a few seconds to soften and seal. Remove carefully and set aside between paper towels. Do this just prior to assembly.

Assembly and Presentation

Put a layer of the combined cheese and onion on a softened tortilla. Top with another tortilla and another layer of cheese and onion, ending with a third tortilla.

▼▼▼

La Hacienda

Pour the sauce on the layered tortillas. Heat in a 350° oven until warm, with the cheese slightly melted.

4 eggs
Pico de Gallo (p. 24)

Meanwhile, either poach or fry the eggs. To serve, top each tortilla stack with an egg. Top with a small spoonful of the cheese mixture and serve with Pico de Gallo.

Storage, Freezing, and Advance Preparation

The sauce may be prepared several days in advance; it freezes well.

Bennie Ferrell Catering, *Houston*   Yield: 6 servings

CHILE QUICHE

This dish could be simplified by using corn tortillas for the crust, as in Bennie Ferrell's Yucatán Quiche (see p. 46). When I first tested this recipe, I thought it too simple and ordinary to include in this book . . . that is, until my son and his food critic friends devoured it. I immediately understood why it is a caterer's favorite!

1 deep-dish pastry shell	Preheat the oven to 400°. Without puncturing the crust, bake the shell for 10 minutes; then remove and cool. Reduce the temperature to 375°. If using a frozen pastry shell, you will need to reduce the half-and-half in the filling, as the prepared shells are smaller. Reduce the cooking time as well by 15 minutes.
2 avocados, mashed 1 clove garlic, minced 3 tablespoons fresh lemon juice 1 tomato, peeled, seeded, and chopped 4 fresh green chiles, roasted and peeled, or 1 4-ounce can mild green chiles (not jalapeños), seeded and chopped ¼ teaspoon hot pepper sauce	In a small bowl, combine the avocados with garlic, lemon juice, tomato, half the chiles, and pepper sauce. Refrigerate until ready to use.
½ pound ground beef ¼ cup onion, chopped 1–2 tablespoons taco-seasoning mix or chile powder	In a medium-size skillet, sauté the beef, onion, remaining chiles and seasoning for about 12 to 15 minutes or until the onion is soft and translucent. Drain and discard all excess fat.
3 eggs, slightly beaten 1½ cups half-and-half ½ teaspoon salt ⅛ teaspoon pepper	In a small bowl, combine the eggs, half-and-half, and seasonings.

Bennie Ferrell's

1½ cups (about 6 ounces) shredded cheddar cheese

Place the grated cheese in the shell, topped by the drained beef and the egg mixture. Bake for 35 to 40 minutes at 375° or until set.

Presentation

chopped tomatoes

Serve the quiche in wedges accompanied by the avocado relish and topped with chopped tomatoes.

shredded lettuce
nacho chips (optional)

Garnish with shredded lettuce and nacho chips, if desired.

Storage, Freezing, and Advance Preparation

This quiche is also as good cold as it is hot, and it makes an excellent picnic item. Prepare it the same day you plan to serve it.

Author's contribution

Yield: 10–12 servings

HUEVOS RANCHEROS

This is a good way to prepare a Mexican breakfast for a crowd, and allow the cook to enjoy his or her guests instead of being trapped in the kitchen. The tortilla cups can be shaped and filled in advance. The black beans are best made at least a day ahead. Purchase a fruit tray from your favorite deli, and your meal is complete.

The Tortillas

½	cup safflower oil
½	stick butter
10–12	thin corn tortillas

Spray large muffin tins with a nonstick vegetable coating spray. Heat the oil and butter in an 8-inch skillet to about 300°. Dip a tortilla for 20–30 seconds, then lift to allow excess oil to run off. Immediately press into muffin tins to make a "cup" shape. Repeat with the remaining tortillas, alternating every other muffin cup.

The Filling

4	ounces spicy pork sausage
¼	cup diced onion
2	tablespoons diced green chiles
4	cups chopped fresh spinach
2–3	tablespoons diced red bell pepper
¼	cup grated Monterey Jack cheese
1	dozen large eggs

To make the filling, saute the pork sausage in a medium skillet over medium-high heat. When browned, add the onion, green chiles, spinach, and red bell pepper, stirring to combine. When the spinach is wilted, remove from the heat and add the cheese. Divide the mixture between the tortilla cups.

Crack an egg on top of each cup and bake at 375° for 20–25 minutes or until the eggs are soft-set and the tortilla edges are lightly browned.

	Black beans (p. 119)
2	cups picante sauce or Roasted Tomato Salsa (p. 29)

Carefully remove the cups and serve with room temperature picante sauce or salsa and Black Beans. Garnish each serving with fresh melon wedges and berries.

▼▼▼

Bennie Ferrell Catering, *Houston*   Yield: 2 servings

GAZPACHO OMELET

Unusual and surprisingly refreshing.

1	tablespoon butter or margarine
¼	cup cucumber, peeled and chopped
¼	cup tomatoes, chopped
2	tablespoons onion, chopped
2	tablespoons green bell pepper, chopped
4	extra large or 6 medium-size eggs
2	tablespoons water
½	teaspoon salt
⅛	teaspoon pepper
	dash of hot pepper sauce
2	tablespoons butter or margarine
½	cup shredded Monterey Jack cheese

In an 8-inch omelet pan or skillet, melt 1 tablespoon butter or margarine. Add the cucumber, tomatoes, onion, and green pepper. Cook over medium-high heat until the onion and pepper are tender, stirring occasionally. Keep warm while preparing omelets.

In a small bowl, combine the eggs, water, salt, pepper, and hot pepper sauce. Beat with a fork or whisk until mixed well but not frothy.

In the same size omelet pan or skillet, melt 1 tablespoon butter or margarine over medium-high heat. When a drop of water sizzles in the pan, pour in half the egg mixture. Cook, gently lifting edges so uncooked portion flows underneath, until eggs are soft but set. Spoon half the vegetable mixture onto omelet, covering only half the omelet. Fold one side over to cover the filling and then slide onto a serving plate. Top with half the cheese and keep warm while preparing the second omelet.

Presentation

Roasted Tomato Salsa
Ninfa's Red Salsa (see p. 22)
chopped avocado

Garnish the omelets with fresh salsa and chopped avocado. Accompany with a medley of fresh fruits such as cantaloupe, honeydew melon, strawberries, and papaya.

Storage, Freezing, and Advance Preparation

The omelets cannot be prepared in advance.

Casa Rosa, *Dallas*   Yield: 6 servings, about 2½ cups Fruit Mix

FRUIT QUESADILLAS

When fresh berries are plentiful, you might prefer to fill the quesadillas with a combination of fresh seasonal berries in place of the cooked fruit combination. In this case, try serving the quesadillas with a warm Cajeta Sauce (see page).

Fruit Mix

½	bag each, frozen whole strawberries, raspberries, and blueberries
⅔	cup sugar
¼	cup cornstarch
½	cup water
6	flour tortillas
9	ounces mascarpone or cream cheese, at room temperature
	butter, melted

To make the Fruit Mix, combine the thawed berries with sugar in a medium saucepan. Dissolve the cornstarch in water and slowly stir into the simmering fruit mixtures. Cook until thickened, about 8–10 minutes. Cool completely.

Soften the tortillas in a hot skillet or microwave oven. Spread one-half of each one with 1½ ounces of the mascarpone or cream cheese. Put about 3 ounces of the fruit mixture on top, fold over and repeat, filling all the tortillas. Brush both sides lightly with melted butter.

Assembly and Presentation

	powdered sugar
6	large fresh strawberries
	mint sprigs
	vanilla ice cream
	Cajeta Sauce (p. 229), (optional)

Heat a large skillet or griddle over medium heat. Cook quesadillas on both sides until lightly browned. Transfer to a dinner plate and sprinkle generously with powdered sugar. Put a scoop of ice cream on top and garnish each plate with a whole strawberry and mint spring. Drizzle warm Cajeta Sauce, if using, over the top.

Advance Preparation

The Fruit Mix may be made several days in advance.

CAPPY'S

Bread (no recipe); *Top right:* Southwestern Cobb Salad (p. 96); *Bottom center:* Grilled Chicken and Black Bean Quesadillas (p. 78), Cornfetti, Mexican Rice (p. 122), Black Beans (p. 119)

APPETIZERS AND SNACKS

ERNESTO'S CEVICHE
Ernesto's

SPINACH CON QUESO
Kokopelli

CAPPY'S CEVICHE
Cappy's

DUCK TAQUITOS
Blue Mesa

DIABLITOS
La Esquina

MOLASSES CURED SALMON TACOS
Boudro's

MEXICAN LAYERED DIP
Bennie Ferrell Catering

LA FOGATA'S RAJAS (CHILE STRIPS)
La Fogata

CRABMEAT NACHOS
Ernesto's

HIGHLAND PARK NACHOS
Mariano's

CRAB AND SHRIMP CAKES
Blue Mesa

QUESO DEL MAR
Ninfa's

GRILLED CHICKEN AND BLACK BEAN
    QUESADILLAS
Cappy's

GOAT CHEESE AND BLACK BEAN
    QUESADILLAS
Author's Contribution

ERNESTO'S CEVICHE

Be sure to use only fresh fish for ceviche. If you are uncertain whether the fish has been frozen, drop it into boiling water for a minute before marinating. I have included several versions of this popular appetizer, each one slightly different.

The Fish

12	medium-size fresh shrimp, peeled and deveined
12	fresh sea scallops

Blanch both shrimp and scallops 1½ minutes in boiling water. Drain and cut in small pieces and place in a glass bowl.

The Sauce

½–¾	cup fresh lime or lemon juice
1	tomato, chopped
1	small yellow onion, chopped
1	jalapeño chile, stemmed, seeded, and diced
2	tablespoons cilantro, chopped
2	tablespoons tomato catsup
5–6	drops Tabasco sauce

Add enough fresh lime or lemon juice to cover, then add vegetables, cilantro, catsup, and Tabasco.

Refrigerate, covered, for at least 3 hours before serving.

Presentation

8	lettuce leaves
1	avocado, sliced
8	tortilla chips

Spoon the ceviche over lettuce leaves and garnish with an avocado slice. Serve with tortilla chips.

Storage, Freezing, and Advance Preparation

The recipe is best prepared a day in advance; it will keep 3 days under refrigeration.

▼▼

Cappy's, *San Antonio*   Yield: 8 servings

CAPPY'S CEVICHE

Cappy uses redfish; however, you may substitute Gulf red snapper, halibut, or swordfish.

The Fish

1	pound fresh sea scallops
1	pound fresh redfish filets
	juice of 8 lemons (about 2 cups)

Cut the scallops and redfish into even pieces, approximately half an inch square. Add to lemon juice, making sure that all the pieces are well coated. Refrigerate in a glass container for 3 to 4 hours or more, stirring occasionally. The lemon juice will "cook" the fish.

The Sauce

½	yellow onion, finely chopped
¼	cup tomato paste
½	cup V-8 juice
1–2	teaspoons salt
½	cup green olives, chopped
2	tablespoons Worcestershire sauce
1	teaspoon Tabasco sauce
3	large tomatoes, seeded and chopped
1	tablespoon fresh parsley, minced
1	tablespoon cilantro, minced
2	serrano chiles, seeded and finely chopped

Meanwhile, using another bowl, combine the sauce ingredients. Stir gently with a spatula until the mixture is uniform. Refrigerate until ready to use.

Using a slotted spoon, remove the fish from its marinade. Discard all but ¾ cup juice. Stir to mix all ingredients and refrigerate.

Presentation

2	heads Bibb lettuce
	snipped cilantro
	sliced avocado
	lime wedges

Serve the ceviche in stemmed martini or margarita glasses, garnished with avocado and fresh lime.

Storage, Freezing, and Advance Preparation

This ceviche may be prepared up to 8 hours in advance, but it should be used within 12 hours.

▼▼

Kokopelli, *Dallas*   Yield 4–5 cups

SPINACH CON QUESO

Serve this with tortilla chips and your favorite tomato salsa. It is a signature dish at Kokopelli.

Spinach

1–2	tablespoons vegetable oil
1	clove garlic, minced
½	white onion, diced
3	cups fresh spinach leaves, chopped
¼	tablespoon cumin
½	jalapeño chile, minced
	salt and pepper

Heat the oil in a medium skillet and sauté garlic, onion, and spinach until wilted and tender, about 6–8 minutes. Add seasonings and mix well. Drain the spinach.

Queso

2	tablespoons chopped green bell pepper
2	tablespoons chopped celery
2	tablespoons chopped green onion
1	jalapeño chile, diced
1	cup water
1½	cups whipping cream
½	cup diced tomatoes
16	ounces cubed Velveeta cheese
4	ounces shredded Cheddar cheese

In a large saucepan bring vegetables and water to a boil. Boil 4–5 minutes or until most of the water evaporates. Stir in cream and bring to a boil. Add the cheeses and tomato and reduce the heat to low. Stir constantly until the cheeses are melted and smooth. Stir in the spinach and transfer the Queso to a crock pot for service.

DUCK TAQUITOS

Taquitos make wonderful appetizers and are not difficult to prepare; however, the duck filling is another matter. I suggest you purchase cooked duck from your favorite Chinese restaurant and limit your time to shredding. If you do not have the Ranchera Sauce prepared, simply use your favorite BBQ sauce, sweetened with 1–2 tablespoons brown sugar, or bring home some duck sauce along with the duck.

The Filling

1–2	tablespoons corn oil
1	pound cooked duck, shredded
1	tablespoon margarine
1	teaspoon pureed garlic
¼	cup minced onions
1	Roma tomato, finely diced
¼	cup diced poblano chile
½	teaspoon leaf oregano
½	teaspoon salt
	pinch black pepper
1	tablespoon minced cilantro

To make the filling, sauté the shredded duck in corn oil. Remove and set aside. Sauté the garlic and onion in hot margarine until lightly browned. Add the tomatoes, poblano chile, seasonings, reserved duck and cilantro and sauté until the mixture is quite dry, about 5–6 minutes.

16–18	thin corn tortillas, preferably blue corn

Soften the corn tortillas by dipping them in 275–300° oil a few seconds to soften. Place a small amount of filling in the center and roll tightly in a cigar shape to enclose the filling. Secure with several toothpicks. Store, covered with plastic wrap until ready to cook.

Blue Mesa

Avocado Sauce

6	tomatillos, rinsed and husked
1	large avocado, peeled, pitted
1	serrano chile, stemmed and seeded
1	clove garlic
1	tablespoon juice from canned jalapeño chiles
1	cup fresh cilantro leaves and upper stems
2	scallions, green and white part

Place all the ingredients for the avocado sauce in a blender jar and blend until smooth.

cold water as needed
salt to taste
fresh lemon juice

Add enough water, as needed, to make a moderately thick and smooth sauce. Season to taste with salt and fresh lemon juice.

Ranchera BBQ Sauce

1	cup mesquite flavored BBQ sauce
½	cup brown sugar
2	cups Ranchera Sauce (p. 36)

Combine the BBQ sauce with Ranchera Sauce and brown sugar over medium heat. Bring to a simmer, stirring constantly. Place both sauces in bowls for dipping.

Bibb or Boston lettuce leaves

When ready to serve, fry the Taquitos 2–3 at a time in 350° peanut oil until crisp, about 30 seconds. Drain on paper towels. Remove the toothpicks and serve on lettuce leaves with both sauces.

La Esquina, *Dallas*   Yield: 3 dozen Diablitos, 2 cups sauce

DIABLITOS

La Esquina makes these little devils with cod; however, you may use any fish fillet such as swordfish or salmon. If you prefer a milder dish, substitute canned green chiles, using a toothpick to enclose the filling.

The Sauce

2	tablespoons all-purpose flour
6	ounces cheddar cheese, finely shredded
4	ounces Monterey Jack cheese, finely shredded
3½	ounces cream cheese, at room temperature
I	cup half-and-half, heated to the boiling point

This sauce is easily made smooth, with consistent results, when a food processor is used. You may use a blender; however, you will need to do the job in 3 batches.

With the metal blade in place, process the flour and cheeses to a paste consistency. With the machine running, pour the hot liquid through the feed tube. Scrape down the sides of the bowl and then transfer mixture to a saucepan; stir constantly over medium heat for 2 to 3 minutes until smooth and thick.

¼	cup onion, chopped
I	tablespoon butter
I	tablespoon pimiento, chopped

In a small skillet, sauté the onion in butter until soft and translucent. Add pimiento and stir into the cheese sauce.

The Chiles

3	dozen jalapeño chiles, stems intact

Rinse the jalapeños. (The jalapeños may be tempered somewhat by a preliminary 30-minute soaking in cold water. Rinse well before stuffing.) Using scissors, make a small slit halfway down each chile, just long enough to allow the filling to be inserted. Cut away the seeds.

La Esquina

The Filling

1	pound grilled swordfish or cod, diced
1	cup ricotta or mild goat cheese
2	tablespoons Parmesan cheese, grated

In a small bowl, blend together the filling ingredients.

2	tablespoons cilantro, chopped
1	teaspoon leaf oregano
¼	teaspoon ground cumin
1–1½	teaspoons salt or to taste
1	tablespoon fresh lime juice
3	tablespoons sour cream

Stuff all the prepared jalapeños. Then either refrigerate until ready to fry or prepare the batter and fry immediately.

The Batter

2	eggs, separated
1–2	tablespoons flour
⅛	teaspoon salt

In a small bowl, beat the egg whites until stiff.

In another bowl, using the same beaters, beat the egg yolks, flour, and salt about a minute until pale yellow and thick. Then beat the yolks into the whites.

Assembly and Presentation

peanut oil for frying

Dip each prepared chile in the batter. Then, using tongs, deep-fry in oil at 375° until crisp and golden, about 1 minute. Drain on a paper towel while preparing the rest of the chiles.

Serve in a chafing dish over hot water with the sauce available for dipping.

La Esquina

Variation

Storage, Freezing, and Advance Preparation

If using the mild green chiles, you may wish to add 1–2 minced jalapeño chiles to the onion and pimiento sauté.

The chiles may be stuffed 8 hours ahead and then refrigerated until you are ready to fry them. When fried, they will keep for about 1 to 2 hours on a warm platter. The sauce may be made several days in advance and refrigerated. It will become quite thick and solid upon refrigeration but melts easily.

▼▼▼

Boudro's, *San Antonio*   Yield: 4 servings

MOLASSES CURED SALMON TACOS

Fish Tacos are common in Mexico and a popular contemporary dish with many Southwestern chefs. The curing process for the salmon is a bit lengthy (but not difficult). A short cut we tried while testing follows the recipe.

Jicama Cole Slaw

1	zucchini squash, julienne
1	large carrot, julienne
1	small jicama, julienne
½	red bell pepper, julienne
1–2	tablespoons fresh lime juice
1–2	tablespoons light olive oil
	salt and pepper to taste

To make the jicama slaw, cut matchstick or julienne strips of the squash, carrot, jicama, and bell pepper. If you have a food processor, use the coarse grating disc. Toss vegetables together and season with equal amounts of lime juice and oil. Add salt and pepper to taste. Chill until ready to serve.

Dressing

1	cup mayonnaise
1	ounce ketchup
2	ounces picante sauce
1	cucumber, thinly sliced
½	red onion, thinly sliced

Combine the mayonnaise, ketchup, and picante sauce and chill. Put the cucumber and onion in a small glass bowl, add ⅓ cup each ice water, white vinegar, and safflower oil. Cover and chill several hours. Drain and sprinkle with salt and pepper.

10–12	ounces fresh salmon, boned and skinned
1	cup kosher salt
¼	cup sugar
2	teaspoons allspice
1	teaspoon cayenne pepper
½	teaspoon nutmeg

To cure the salmon, combine the dry seasonings and rub on both sides of the fish. Wrap in plastic wrap, then foil, and refrigerate for 24 hours.

▼▼

Boudro's

¼   cup soy sauce
1   cup molasses

Mix together the soy sauce and molasses. Unwrap the fish and drain the water. Brush the fish on both sides with the molasses mix. Wrap again in plastic wrap and foil and refrigerate for another 24 hours.

Unwrap the fish and place on a rack, uncovered, and refrigerate to dry for 48 hours.

Place the rack on a cookie sheet so the moisture can drain.

6   flour tortillas

To serve, put the dressing, Jicama Slaw, and cucumber-onion mixture in separate bowls. Thinly slice the salmon and put it on a serving plate with the warm tortillas and sprigs of fresh cilantro.

Put a little dressing on each tortilla with jicama slaw, salmon, and cucumber and onions. Fold and eat like a taco.

Note: A quick version is to grill the salmon and "flake" it coarsely. Serve the warm salmon and tortillas with the same accompaniments. To grill, combine ¼ cup soy sauce with ½ cup molasses and about ¼ teaspoon cayenne pepper. Brush the salmon with this mixture while grilling, brushing both sides. Grill about 8 minutes per inch of thickness.

Cool the salmon for about 3–4 minutes. Using two forks, "flake" the meat and serve with accompaniments.

Bennie Ferrell Catering, *Houston*   Yield: 8–10 servings

Mexican Layered dip

This popular layered appetizer is always the first to disappear at a party. Simple to prepare and perfect to take to a party.

3	avocados
1	clove garlic, minced
2	tablespoons fresh lemon juice
1	teaspoon salt
	white pepper to taste

With a fork, mash the avocados with garlic and lemon juice, and then season with salt and white pepper. Spread half in a 9-inch pie pan.

1	small yellow onion, chopped
2	tomatoes, chopped
1	cup (about 4 ounces) grated cheddar cheese

Top with onion, tomatoes, and cheese, then with the remaining avocado.

½	cup cooked chile con carne
¾	cup refried beans

Combine and heat the chile and beans and then add atop the avocado.

1	cup sour cream
1	cup green chiles (optional)
1	cup (about 4 ounces) grated Monterey Jack cheese

Spoon the sour cream and green chiles, if desired, over the bean mixture. Top with Monterey Jack cheese.

tortilla chips

Serve at room temperature with tortilla chips.

Storage, Freezing, and Advance Preparation

You may make this ahead by preparing all the ingredients early in the day and assembling the dish about 1 hour before serving.

La Fogata, *San Antonio*   Yield: 6–8 servings

La Fogata's Rajas (Chile Strips)

Positively, this is the best appetizer anywhere, anytime. It is also good as a sauce for chicken or fish.

6	poblano chiles, roasted and peeled
1	onion, halved and cut in strips
2–3	tablespoons vegetable oil
8	ounces cream cheese, cut in 4–5 pieces
½	teaspoon garlic powder
	pinch of ground cumin
	salt to taste
6–8	ounces Oaxaca or mozzarella cheese, grated

Stem and seed the chiles and cut into narrow strips.

Sauté the onion in vegetable oil until soft and translucent, about 5 to 8 minutes. Do not brown. Add the chiles and cook 1 minute, then add the cream cheese and spices. When the cream cheese is completely melted, add the grated Oaxaca or mozzarella cheese in 6 to 8 handfuls. Allow the cheese to melt without stirring and take care to keep the temperature low.

Assembly

6–8	hot flour tortillas

Serve in individual ramekins with a hot flour tortilla draped over the top of each bowl. To eat, the raja mixture is simply spooned into the tortilla, which is rolled or folded to keep the mixture from spilling out. Remember the trick of tipping one end up so you don't lose any of the delicious filling.

Storage, Freezing, and Advance Preparation

The chile and onion mixture may be prepared up to 2 days in advance and either refrigerated or frozen until ready to use. Be sure to reheat it before adding the two cheeses.

CRABMEAT NACHOS

Ernesto uses snow crab in his restaurant, but he says nachos made with lump crabmeat are very special. The smooth and creamy butter sauce has become his specialty. Carefully follow the directions, and never allow the butter to simmer or lose its creamy look.

2	scallions, thinly sliced
I	clove garlic, minced
I	stick unsalted butter, at room temperature
I	large tomato, peeled and chopped
I	serrano chile, minced
I	tablespoon cilantro, snipped

In a medium-size to small skillet, sauté the scallions and garlic in 1 tablespoon butter until softened. Do not allow the butter to brown. Then stir in the tomato, chile, and cilantro. Reduce the heat to low and, about 1 tablespoon at a time, whisk in the rest of the softened butter. Whisk until creamy; do not allow the butter to simmer at any time. Lift the pan from the heat if necessary to control the temperature. You may hold the sauce over a pan of hot water until ready to use.

1¾	cups cooked crabmeat
¼	cup dry sherry or vermouth

Heat the crabmeat in sherry or vermouth for a few seconds. Stir in about 1 cup of the prepared sauce and then set aside.

Assembly and Presentation

20	nacho chips
8	ounces Monterey Jack cheese, grated

To assemble, place crabmeat mixture on each nacho and cover with cheese. Place 4 to 6 inches from the broiler for 3 to 5 minutes or until the cheese is melted.

I	avocado, diced
20	slices jalapeño chiles (optional)

Garnish with a few pieces of diced avocado and, if desired, a jalapeño slice.

Variation

You may add a cooked and halved shrimp to each nacho if desired.

Storage, Freezing, and Advance Preparation

The sauce may be prepared in advance and held over hot water (off the heat) for about an hour.

▼▼

Mariano's, *Dallas*   Yield: 1 dozen nachos

HIGHLAND PARK NACHOS

Practically every restaurant in Texas has a version of these "Nachos Rancheros"; however, these are particularly interesting because of the jalapeño relish.

2 cups leftover beef, cooked and chopped, or skirt steak, charcoal-grilled and cut in bite-size pieces	Warm the meat, or if using leftover steak, place under the broiler a few minutes to heat.
1 4-ounce can jalapeño chiles, packed with carrots and onions	Strain the carrots and onions from the jalapeños and then stem and seed the chiles. Finely chop all the vegetables, then combine with the tomato and cilantro.
1 large tomato, peeled and finely chopped	
2 tablespoons cilantro, minced	

Assembly and Presentation

1 dozen nacho chips, preferably flat triangles	Place the chips on an ovenproof platter. Spread each chip with 1–2 teaspoons beans. Cover the chips completely with grated cheese, so that there are no chips showing through the beans and cheese. Put the chips under the broiler until the cheese melts.
½–1 cup refried beans	
1 cup cheddar cheese, grated	
1 cup Guacamole (see p. 32)	
½ cup sour cream	

Remove from oven and cover with 1–2 teaspoons Guacamole, a dollop of sour cream, 1–2 teaspoons of the relish, and then pieces of skirt steak or leftover beef.

Storage, Freezing, and Advance Preparation

All the ingredients may be prepared in advance; however, the assembly and baking should be done just prior to serving.

▼▼▼

Mesa, Houston   Yield: 14–16

CRAB AND SHRIMP CAKES

Blue Mesa combines fresh crab and shrimp to make their crab cakes. The two sauces make a colorful plate and are worth the effort. We tested this recipe using lobster and crab as well as a combination shrimp, lobster, and crab . . . feel free to substitute.

2	large eggs
1	cup mayonnaise
¼	teaspoon black pepper
¼	teaspoon cayenne pepper
1	teaspoon paprika
1½	teaspoon dry mustard powder
1½	teaspoon celery seed, crushed
1	teaspoon salt
½	teaspoon Tabasco
½	tablespoon Worcestershire Sauce
2	pounds crab meat (claw or lump)
½	pound cooked, diced shrimp
¾	cup diced onions
1½	cups fresh bread crumbs

Beat the eggs in a large mixing bowl and whip in all the ingredients except shellfish, onions, and bread crumbs. Gently fold these in last, being careful to keep pieces of crab as large as possible. Form into cakes about 3 ounces each. Refrigerate until ready to cook.

Cilantro Cream Sauce

3	ounces white wine
1	ounce white wine vinegar
¼	cup diced onion
1	clove garlic, minced
¼	cup finely minced cilantro
⅓	cup whipping cream
½	pound unsalted butter, in pieces
	salt and pepper to taste

Red Bell Pepper Sauce (p. 37)

To make the Cilantro Cream Sauce, bring the wine, vinegar, onion, garlic, and cilantro to a boil in a medium saucepan. Boil for 3–4 minutes, or until the liquid is reduced by about half. Add the cream and continue to boil about 4–5 more minutes, or until thickened. Reduce the heat to medium-low and, in several batches, slowly whip in the butter pieces. Do not allow the butter to separate. Remove the pan from the heat, if necessary, to keep the sauce from breaking. Season to taste with salt and pepper. Strain the sauce. Keep the sauce warm in a double boiler until ready to use.

Sauté the crab and shrimp cakes in hot butter until golden brown and fully heated. Pool both sauces on a serving plate and serve 1 to 2 cakes per person.

Yield: 2–4 servings

QUESO DEL MAR

2   tablespoons onion, chopped
I   strip bacon, cut in several
    pieces

In a large skillet that may be transferred to the oven, sauté the onion and bacon until the bacon is lightly browned, about 5 to 6 minutes. Pour off excess fat.

I   medium-size tomato, peeled
    and chopped
¼   teaspoon garlic powder
    dash of black pepper

Add the tomato and spices to the onion mixture.

4   jumbo shrimp, peeled and
    deveined, coarsely chopped
3–4 tablespoons whipping cream

Add the shrimp and simmer for 1 to 2 minutes. Stir in the cream and bring to a boil.

8   ounces Monterey Jack cheese,
    grated, at room temperature

Add the grated cheese to the skillet, tossing to combine. Immediately transfer to a preheated 350° oven and bake for 3 to 5 minutes or until the cheese is melted. Stir briefly with a spoon to ensure that the vegetables and shrimp are evenly distributed throughout the cheese. Take care to watch the heat and do not stir except very briefly or the cheese will clump together.

If using a microwave oven, combine the grated cheese with the shrimp and vegetables and place in a dish. Microwave on high for 1 minute or until the cheese is melted.

Assembly

4   hot flour or corn tortillas

To serve, place 2 tablespoons of the shrimp-cheese mixture in each tortilla and roll it up like a flute, turning the end up to prevent the filling from escaping.

Storage, Freezing, and Advance Preparation

This is best when made just prior to serving.

▼▼▼

Cappy's, *San Antonio*   Yield: 4 servings, 2 per person

GRILLED CHICKEN AND BLACK BEAN QUESADILLAS

Cappy prepares his quesadillas with a roasted tomato salsa, adding a rich, grilled flavor to the quesadillas. You can use your favorite tomato salsa or the Roasted Tomato Salsa on page 29. These are hearty enough to make as an entrée, or cut each one in thirds and serve as an appetizer.

3	3–3½-ounce boneless chicken breasts
	vegetable oil, or light olive oil
	salt and pepper

Cook the chicken on an outdoor grill, or sauté over medium-high heat in a skillet. Brush both sides of the chicken with vegetable or light olive oil and season with salt and pepper. Cook on both sides until lightly browned, about 6–7 minutes. Cut the chicken into a small dice, reserving all juices.

8	flour tortillas
1	cup pureed black beans
4	ounces grated longhorn cheddar cheese
4	ounces grated Monterey Jack cheese
¾–1	cup Corn and Black Bean Relish (p. 28)
½	cup thinly sliced red onion, seared
½	cup Cornfetti (p. 97)
¾	cup tomato salsa

Soften the tortillas in a microwave oven or hot skillet. Spread the black bean puree thinly over half of each tortilla. Top with diced chicken, a spoonful of each cheese, the corn relish, onion rings, and a few strips of Cornfetti. Drizzle with the salsa. Fold over and gently press down to enclose the filling.

Grill the quesadillas in a nonstick skillet or griddle, brushed lightly with olive oil on both sides. Keep cooked quesadillas warm in a 300° oven while cooking the rest.

The Presentation

Guacamole (p. 32)
Pico de Gallo (p. 24)

Cut into wedges and serve with Guacamole and Pico de Gallo.

▼▼

Author's Contribution   Yield: 8 quesadillas (24 wedges)

GOAT CHEESE AND BLACK BEAN QUESADILLAS

1½ cups Papaya Pico de Gallo (p. 24)	Prepare the Pico de Gallo. Add 1 cup diced, fresh papaya. Chill until ready to use.
Refried Black Beans (p. 115)	Prepare the Refried Black Beans and set aside.
8 7–8-inch flour tortillas	Soften the tortillas one at a time in a hot skillet or microwave oven. Spread half the tortillas with Black Bean Puree. Drain all juices from the Papaya Pico de Gallo and put 1–2 tablespoons on top of the beans.
12 ounces mild, American goat cheese	Cut the goat cheese in very thin slices and put on top of the Papaya Pico de Gallo. Fold over to seal. Repeat with the remaining torillas. Cover with plastic wrap until ready to cook. Heat a large saute pan to medium-high (or use a griddle). Lightly brush both sides of the quesadillas with melted butter and cook on both sides until lightly browned. (Hold cooked quesadillas in a 250° oven while preparing the rest).
Chile Arbol Sauce (p. 43) Guacamole (p. 32)	Cut into 3 or 4 wedges and serve with Chile Arbol Sauce and Guacamole.

EL MIRADOR
El Mirador's soups (pp. 80, 84–85, 86–87, and 89)

SOUPS

EL MIRADOR'S MEXICAN SOUP
El Mirador

TORTILLA SOUP
The Mansion on Turtle Creek

ROASTED CORN CHOWDER
Blue Mesa

FRIDAY'S BEAN SOUP
El Mirador

CALDO DE RES
El Mirador

PUMPKIN SOUP WITH SPICED PEANUTS
Author's Contribution

SOPA DE FIDEO
El Mirador

CHICKEN POBLANO CHOWDER
Casa Rosa

DRUNKEN BLACK BEAN SOUP
Cappy's

BLACK BEAN SOUP
Casa Rosa

BLACK BEAN CHILE
Casa Rosa

▼▼

El Mirador, *San Antonio*   Yield: 8 servings

EL MIRADOR'S MEXICAN SOUP

This is the soup that brings crowds to El Mirador each weekend. Mary begins her preparation two days in advance.

The Stock

2½	quarts water
5	cloves garlic
3	fresh oregano sprigs
2	whole cloves
1	tablespoon salt
1	tablespoon ground cumin
1	teaspoon pepper
3	bay leaves, broken
1–2	basil sprigs (omit if fresh basil is not available)
5	chicken bouillon cubes
1	3-pound frying chicken, cut up

Bring the water to a boil, and then add all the ingredients, including the chicken. Skim the foam from the top as the soup simmers for 1 to 1½ hours. Remove the chicken, debone it, and shred the meat when cool. Then, strain the stock and chill. This hardens the fat for easy removal.

The Vegetables

	juice of 2 limes
1	medium-size zucchini, chopped
1	yellow onion, sliced
2	stalks celery, chopped
1	carrot, chopped
1	green bell pepper, seeded and chopped
1	17-ounce can garbanzo beans, drained

The day you plan to serve the soup, reheat the defatted stock and add the juice of 2 limes. Add the vegetables and cook just until tender-crisp, about 20 minutes. Add the shredded chicken and garbanzo beans.

Presentation

	Mexican Rice (p. 122) (optional)
2	avocados, sliced
	Salsa (p. 31)

To serve the soup, ladle into large soup bowls (over the rice, if using). Garnish with sliced avocados and fresh salsa.

Storage, Freezing, and Advance Preparation

The stock may be made 1 to 2 days ahead.

The Mansion on Turtle Creek, *Dallas*

Yield: 4 servings

TORTILLA SOUP

While there is nothing Mexican-American about the Mansion, it was the first elegant restaurant to incorporate "Texas" items or offer traditional Mexican American or Southwestern specialties. The soup is an adaptation of the tortilla soup served at the Argyle Club in San Antonio. The Mansion's upscale presentation of Texas food has encouraged others to do the same, and the result will be more Southwestern specialties in fine Dallas restaurants.

3	corn tortillas
	vegetable oil or peanut oil for frying
	salt to taste

Cut the tortillas in short julienne strips. Heat about 3 inches of oil to 375 to 400°. Fry the tortilla strips a few at a time for about 45 seconds or until crisp. Drain on paper towels and add salt to taste. Set aside.

1	ancho chile, stemmed and seeded

Simmer the chile in enough hot water to cover until softened. Drain and discard water.

1	1-pound can tomatoes, coarsely chopped, including juice
2	cloves garlic
½	cup onion, chopped
1–2	tablespoons corn oil
8	cups chicken stock
1	teaspoon, more or less, ground cumin
1	teaspoon white pepper
	salt to taste
3–4	tablespoons tomato sauce, if needed

In a blender, puree the ancho chile and tomatoes with the garlic and onion. Transfer to a 3-quart saucepan and sauté in hot oil for 5 to 10 minutes. Add chicken stock and seasonings and simmer, uncovered, for 30 to 45 minutes or until reduced and flavorful. Adjust seasonings to taste, adding tomato sauce and more cumin if desired.

The Mansion on Turtle Creek

Assembly and Presentation

1	avocado, diced
8	ounces cheddar cheese, grated
	shredded chicken (optional)

When ready to serve, reheat the broth. Place the garnishes (tortilla strips, avocado, and cheese) in small bowls to be served with the soup.

Storage, Freezing, and Advance Preparation

The stock may be made several days in advance and, if desired, frozen.

▼▼▼

Blue Mesa, *Dallas*   Yield: 6–8 servings

ROASTED CORN CHOWDER

The soup pictured on page 94 is a two-colored soup, using Black Bean and Roasted Corn. There are two Black Bean Soups to choose from on pp. 91 and 92; however, they are not from Blue Mesa. Whichever Black Bean Soup you use, this makes a colorful appetizer that is sure to please everyone.

5 ears fresh corn, in the husk	Heat the oven to 400°. Rinse the husks with water and place them on cookie sheets. (If the husk has been partially removed, wrap the ear of corn in foil). Roast for 50 minutes. Cool and remove the husk. Cut the kernels from the cob and set aside.

1½ cups chicken broth
1½ cups whipping cream
½ pound Velveeta cheese, in pieces
⅛ cup (canned) finely minced jalapeños
salt to taste

Put all but ½ cup of the kernels in a blender and puree with the chicken broth. Heat the corn puree and whipping cream in a large saucepan over medium heat and simmer for 10 minutes. Stir in the cheese, whole corn, and jalapeños and cook, stirring constantly, until the cheese has melted. Add salt to taste.

If the soup thickens when reheating, thin with a little chicken broth.

Black Bean Soup (pp. 91 or 92)
¾ cup Pico de Gallo (p. 24)
¾ cup sour cream

To serve the soup, pour equal amounts of both the Black Bean soup and Corn Chowder (at the same time) into a soup bowl. Garnish the Black Bean side with a drizzle of sour cream, the Corn Chowder side with Pico de Gallo.

▼▼▼

El Mirador, *San Antonio*   Yield: 8–10 servings

Sopa Tarasca

This soup gets its name from the Michoacán Indians in Mexico, who lived near the famous lake and used butterfly nets for fishing. Sopa Tarasca is a good way to use leftover beans and taste anything but leftover. Mary often calls it "Friday's Soup."

The Bean Broth

3½–4	cups whole pinto beans, including juice
2	14½-ounce cans chicken or beef stock
1	teaspoon salt or to taste

Combine the beans with stock and salt to taste. Bring to a simmer, using a 2½-quart saucepan, then reduce heat and keep warm while preparing the salsa vegetables.

The Salsa Vegetables

1–2	tablespoons vegetable oil
5–6	tomatoes, quartered
4	cloves garlic, minced
1	medium-size onion, diced
2–3	chile ancho or pasilla pods, stemmed and seeded
	pinch of cumin
	salt and pepper to taste
2	bay leaves

Put 1–2 tablespoons of vegetable oil in a heavy-duty skillet large enough to hold the tomatoes, garlic, onion, and chile pods. Season with the cumin, salt, and pepper. Cook over medium to medium-low heat 20 to 25 minutes or until the onions and tomatoes are very soft. When the salsa vegetables are tender, puree the mixture in a blender. Then cook the salsa mixture with the bay leaves for just a few minutes, using the same skillet. Discard the bay leaves. Add this mixture to the bean broth and adjust seasonings to taste. The soup is not extremely thick—thin with additional stock if necessary and taste to adjust seasonings.

▼▼

El Mirador

Assembly and Presentation

| 1 | dozen tortillas, preferably fresh |
| | peanut oil for frying |

Cut the tortillas in narrow strips and spread on a cookie sheet to dry out. Deep-fry in several batches until crisp. If the strips do not dry out before frying, they tend to foam up; therefore, small batches are recommended.

| 4–6 | ounces Monterey Jack cheese, grated |
| 1 | tablespoon sour cream per serving |

In a serving bowl, place a few tortilla strips and some cheese, and then cover with the soup. Garnish with sour cream dollops.

Variation

I like to add minced cilantro and crumbled bacon, making a ranchero-style bean soup. Canned ranch-style beans may be substituted for fresh-cooked pintos.

Storage, Freezing and Advance Preparation

Both the tortilla strips and the salsa vegetables may be made in advance; then you can make soup using leftover beans or have a quick, hearty meal using canned beans.

▼▼▼

El Mirador, *San Antonio*   Yield: 8–10 servings

CALDO DE RES

This is a hearty beef soup, typical of the northern Mexican style. It is not highly seasoned, as it is meant to be served with fresh salsas, the salt and pepper of Texas tables.

The Meat Broth

1½	quarts water
1	14½-ounce can beef stock
½–1	pound beef brisket, cut in 2–3 pieces
2	beef shanks (about ¼ pound)
2	cloves garlic, minced
½	teaspoon ground cumin

Bring the water and beef stock to a boil. Add beef and return to a boil. Skim the foam that rises to the top and discard. Add the garlic and cumin, and simmer 1½ to 2 hours. When the beef is tender, remove the meat from the bones; discard the bones and fat. Skim all visible fat; this is easier to do when the soup is chilled. Place the soup in the freezer for 1 hour, then the fat is easily removed. Coarsely shred all the meat and set aside.

The Vegetables

2	carrots, cut in matchstick strips
1	turnip, cut in matchstick strips
1	small onion, thinly sliced
1	bell pepper, cut in matchstick strips
⅓	head green cabbage, thinly sliced
2	stalks celery, cut in matchstick strips
1	zucchini, cut in matchstick strips
5–6	cilantro sprigs and/or 3 mint sprigs
	salt and pepper to taste

Cut the vegetables of your choice into matchstick strips, 2½ by ¼ inches. Return the broth to a boil and add the shredded meat, carrots, turnip, onion, and bell pepper. Cook 5 to 6 minutes. After a few minutes, add the remaining vegetables and the herbs of your choice. Adjust seasonings. Cook just long enough to make all the vegetables tender-crisp, about 2 more minutes.

▼▼

El Mirador

Assembly and Presentation

6   corn tortillas
     peanut oil for frying
     salt
     Salsa (see p. 31)
     Green Chile Salsa (see p. 23)
     Pico de Gallo (see p. 24)

Cut the tortillas into thin julienne strips and deep-fry in several batches until crisp. If the oil foams, you have fried too many at one time—either air-dry the strips 2 to 3 hours to remove moisture or fry in smaller batches.

Lightly salt and serve with the soup along with salsas.

Storage, Freezing, and Advance Preparation

The broth may be prepared a day in advance. Adjust salt and pepper in the soup when reheating.

PUMPKIN SOUP WITH SPICED PEANUTS

This soup is as good chilled as it is hot.

1½	pounds fresh pumpkin, peeled, seeds and strings removed, or equal amounts cooked and pureed winter squash (acorn or butternut) and canned pumpkin
½	stick unsalted butter
1	tablespoon flour

In a medium-size saucepan, cook the fresh pumpkin until very tender, about 15 to 20 minutes. In a blender, puree the pumpkin along with the butter and flour. If using winter squash, peel, seed, and cook the same way.

2	14½-ounce cans chicken stock
½	cup whole milk

Bring the chicken stock and milk to a boil. Stir in the pumpkin and winter squash, if using, and return to a boil. Reduce heat immediately. Blend again if you want a smoother soup.

1	cup heavy cream
1½	teaspoons salt
¼	teaspoon white pepper
¼–½	teaspoon cayenne pepper (to taste)

Stir in the cream and then season with salt, pepper, and cayenne. Allow the soup to simmer and thicken for 30 to 40 minutes, stirring occasionally. Keep warm until ready to serve or refrigerate and serve when chilled.

Presentation

spiced hot peanuts or roasted, hulled and salted pumpkin seeds
minced cilantro

Garnish the hot or cold soup with spiced peanuts or pumpkin seeds and minced cilantro. Spiced hot peanuts are available in many stores that carry specialty Mexican foods.

Storage, Freezing, and Advance Preparation

The soup may be made 1 to 2 days in advance. It freezes well; however, it may need vigorous whisking when thawed.

▼▼

El Mirador, *San Antonio*   Yield: 6 servings

Sopa de Fideo

This is actually more of a side dish than a soup. The addition of 3 to 4 more cups of chicken or beef stock will make a more soup-like consistency. I urge you to add seasoned chorizo or East Texas sausage to the sautéed onions and garlic. This is a mildy seasoned dish which is easily spiced, if desired, with minced jalapeño.

8 ounces vermicelli, broken in small pieces 2–3 tablespoons oil, heated	In a large skillet, over medium heat, sauté the vermicelli in hot oil. Watch carefully since it burns easily; however, be sure all the pieces are browned.
4 tomatoes, cores intact 1 yellow onion, cut in 4–5 pieces 2 cloves garlic, unpeeled	Place the tomatoes, onion, and garlic on an oiled cookie sheet 4 inches from the broiling element. Leave the door ajar and cook until charred and caramelized. Cool and peel the garlic, and then puree the vegetables and all their juices in a blender.
2 cups, more or less, chicken stock, preferably homemade	Immediately add the blended tomato, onion, and garlic mixture to the vermicelli with enough stock to achieve a soupy consistency.
1 bunch green onions, chopped 1 clove garlic, minced 2 tablespoons vegetable oil 2 bell peppers, chopped or sliced (use red or green peppers or a combination of both) ½ cup cilantro leaves, snipped, or 2 mint sprigs salt and pepper to taste	In a separate skillet, sauté the onions and garlic in oil 2 minutes. Stir in the peppers and cilantro or mint and adjust liquid as necessary. Add salt and pepper to taste. Add the onion-pepper mixture to the vermicelli.

Presentation

2–3 ounces Parmesan cheese, grated	Serve garnished with Parmesan cheese.

Yield: 5–8 servings

CHICKEN POBLANO CHOWDER

Fresh grilled corn gives the soup a smoky, distinctive flavor. It may be served as an appetizer soup or light entrée. Casa Rosa serves it with grated cheese and sour cream.

3	2½–3 ounce boneless, skinless chicken breasts

Preheat an indoor or outdoor grill to the highest setting. Lightly brush the chicken breasts with oil, season with salt and pepper, and grill on both sides until browned, about 8–10 minutes total cooking time. Cut the chicken into ¼-inch pieces.

1½	cups grilled or roasted corn kernels

Grill 2–3 ears of corn in the same manner. Cool and cut kernels from the cob. Set both chicken and corn aside. Both may be grilled 6–8 inches from the broiling element in your oven; increase the cooking time 4–5 minutes.

2	tablespoons butter or margarine
2	strips lean bacon, diced
1	clove garlic, minced
1¼	cups diced onion
¼	cup diced celery
1	cup diced poblano chiles, roasted and peeled
1	cup diced red bell pepper
1	cup diced carrots
5	tablespoons all-purpose flour
1	teaspoon ground cumin
¼	teaspoon garlic powder
¼	teaspoon leaf oregano
¼	teaspoon white pepper
1	teaspoon black pepper
1⅓	cups milk
1	14½-ounce can chicken broth salt to taste
2	tablespoons chopped cilantro

Heat the butter and diced bacon in a large skillet over medium-high heat. Sauté until bacon is lightly browned. Add garlic and onion and sauté until translucent. Add the celery, chiles, peppers, and carrots and cook 3–4 minutes. Sprinkle the flour and all seasonings evenly over the vegetables, stirring constantly. Slowly add the milk and chicken broth, in small amounts. Cook, stirring constantly, until smooth and thickened, about 5–8 minutes. Add salt to taste, cilantro, and reserved chicken and corn.

Serve the soup hot with grated cheese and sour cream on the side.

▼▼

Cappy's, *San Antonio*   Yield: 12 servings

DRUNKEN BLACK BEAN SOUP

Borracho Beans came from the haciendas of Mexico. The kitchens of the large ranches were pressed to provide food 24 hours a day. Often the cooks had to work through the night while the owner of the ranch and his family and other workers slept. During those nighttime hours, the cooks liked to take a little nip of beer or wine. As the story goes, on one occasion the cook got careless and spilled beer into the beans. When the owner tasted the beans the next day, he commended the cook on the new seasoning. The beans were dubbed drunken beans.

1	pound dried black beans	Wash, drain, and pick through beans to remove stones and/or spoiled beans.
9–10	cups chicken stock	
		In a large stockpot, bring the chicken stock and beans to a boil.
¼	pound bacon, chopped	In a medium-size skillet or sauté pan, sauté the bacon with onion and garlic, until the bacon is lightly browned. Add to the beans and cook over medium heat about an hour, or until the beans are just tender and the stock has thickened.
1	onion, diced	
1	clove garlic, minced	
2–3	tablespoons tomato paste	Add the tomato paste, salt, and pepper, being careful not to get the soup too salty. Adjust seasonings to taste as necessary.
½–1	teaspoon salt	
¼–½	teaspoon pepper	
½–1	tablespoon cilantro, minced	Stir in cilantro and beer and continue cooking 1 to 1½ hours. The soup should have an abundant amount of broth; be prepared to add more chicken stock if necessary.
1	cup beer	
	grated Monterey Jack cheese Pico de Gallo (p. 24)	Serve the soup with grated cheese and Pico de Gallo.

Casa Rosa, *Dallas*

Yield: 8 servings

BLACK BEAN SOUP

Casa Rosa's Black Bean Soup is made without fat of any kind, and has wonderful flavor from all the vegetables and seasonings. If you miss a "meaty" flavor you can add some diced bacon, ham hock, or ham bone. This is the base for their Black Bean Chile.

2	cups black beans	Clean beans for rocks and other objects and soak for 1–2 hours.
8	cups (more or less) water	Put the beans in a large saucepan or stock pot with water and bring to a boil. Add remaining ingredients, except cilantro and salt, and cook 2–2½ hours, or until beans are soft.
1	cup diced onions	
¼	cup diced celery	
½	cup diced carrots	
¼	cup tomato paste	
1	bay leaf	
1	clove garlic, minced	
¼	teaspoon ground oregano	
¼	teaspoon crushed red pepper	
1	tablespoon minced cilantro	Add cilantro and salt to taste. The soup should be moderately thick.
1½–2	teaspoons salt, or to taste	

Garnish and Presentation

Pico de Gallo (p. 24) grated cheese or crumbled goat cheese	Use the soup to make Black Bean Chile (p. 93) or serve garnished with Pico de Gallo, sour cream, and grated cheese.

▼▼▼

Casa Rosa, *Dallas*   Yield: 6 cups

BLACK BEAN CHILE

Casa Rosa's Black Bean Chile is made from their Black Bean Soup in which the beans are whole rather than pureed.

1 pound lean sirloin or top round	Trim the sirloin or top round, removing all silver skin. Cut into ½-inch cubes.
4–5 strips bacon, diced 2–3 cloves garlic, minced 1½ tablespoons chile powder 1 teaspoon cumin ½ teaspoon paprika 1 teaspoon crushed red pepper ¼ teaspoon ground oregano	In a large saucepan, sauté bacon and garlic until bacon is lightly browned. Add the beef and continue to cook until beef is browned and juices no longer run pink. Add all seasonings except salt and simmer 6–8 minutes.
4 cups Black Bean Soup (p. 92) water as needed ½–1 teaspoon salt, or to taste	Add the soup and simmer 10–15 minutes, adding water to thin, if necessary. Season to taste with salt.

Garnish and Presentation

1 cup cooked corn kernels 1 cup diced tomatoes or Pico de Gallo (p. 24) fresh minced cilantro	Serve the chile in bowls garnished with fresh corn, diced tomatoes, or Pico de Gallo and fresh minced cilantro.

BLUE MESA

Left: Grilled Chicken and Corn Pasta (p. 188); *Rear:* Southwestern Caesar Salad (p. 100); *Right:* Chicken and Mushroom Enchiladas with Tomatillo Sauce (p. 132), Corn Cake, Black Beans, and Grilled Vegetables; Adobe Pie (pp. 156–157); *Bottom:* Chicken Fajitas (pp. 204–205); *Center:* Roasted Corn Chowder Black Bean Soup (p. 83)

SALADS

SOUTHWESTERN COBB SALAD
Cappy's

CORNFETTI SALAD WITH AVOCADO RANCH
Cappy's

JICAMA SALAD
Casa Rosa

RADISH-CUCUMBER SALAD WITH PUMPKIN SEED AND GOAT CHEESE
Mark Gonzales

SOUTHWESTERN CAESAR SALAD
Mesa

NOPALITO SALAD
El Mirador

BLACKENED TUNA SALAD WITH CRISPY WALNUTS
Z-Tejas

SANGRÍA MOUSSE
Bennie Ferrell Catering

SMOKED CHICKEN SALAD WITH CHIPOTLE RANCH DRESSING
Mark Gonzales

SHRIMP AND JICAMA SLAW WITH CHIPOTLE RANCH DRESSING
Author's Contribution

POLLO SALAD
Cafe Noche

SOUTHWESTERN COBB SALAD

This is a colorful and delicious "take" on the traditional Cobb Salad. It has become one of the most popular items on Cappy's menu. Many restaurants use a "field green" mix that is available in some grocery stores. If not, use your favorite combination of lettuces.

The Marinade

1	cup light vegetable oil
1	cup Thai Chile Sauce
½	cup fresh lime juice
⅔	cup soy sauce
⅓	cup ketchup

Combine the marinade ingredients and mix well. Transfer to a glass casserole dish. Marinate the chicken for 2–3 hours.

4	chicken breasts, skinless, boneless
	salt and pepper

Preheat an indoor or outdoor grill to the highest setting. Remove the chicken from the marinade and grill on both sides for about 6–8 minutes total time or roast the chicken in a 375° oven for 12–15 minutes. Shred or cut the chicken into bite-size pieces.

	Avocado Ranch Dressing (p. 97)
10–12	cups mixed greens
	Guacamole (p. 32)
	Corn and Black Bean Relish (p. 28)
	Pico de Gallo (p. 24)
	Cotija cheese
	Cornfetti (p. 97)

Toss the greens with about ⅔ cup of the dressing. Divide between four large plates. Arrange the chicken, Corn and Black Bean Relish, and Cornfetti, in rows atop the greens. Place Guacamole and Pico de Gallo in the center. Serve additional dressing with each salad.

▼▼

Cappy's, *San Antonio*   Yield: 6 salads

Cornfetti Salad With Avocado Ranch

You may use the prepacked salad greens, choosing from "field" or "gourmet" combinations or the "Italian" mix. Cappy uses guacamole in his recipe, but for ease of preparation, I've used avocado, lemon, and garlic and suggested a garnish from the remaining avocado.

Cornfetti

4	yellow corn tortillas
4	blue corn tortillas
4	red corn tortillas
	peanut or corn oil
	salt

Using a sharp knife, cut the tortillas in half. Turn one-quarter and cut each half into very thin, short strips. Let the strips stand at room temperature 30–45 minutes to "dry-out."

Heat 2–3 inches of oil in a deep saucepan to 350°. Fry the strips in several batches, using a deep strainer or basket to contain all the strips. Fry until crisp, about 30–45 seconds. Remove and drain on towels. Sprinkle with salt immediately. Store in tightly covered containers or zip-lock bags.

Avocado Ranch Dressing

3	cups Ranch dressing
2	tablespoons fresh minced cilantro
1	small clove garlic, peeled
1	avocado, divided use
1–2	teaspoons fresh lemon juice
1	tablespoon minced sweet onion
1	small head red-tip leaf lettuce, rinsed
½	head iceberg lettuce, rinsed
½	head Romaine lettuce, rinsed
4	Roma tomatoes, diced
6–8	ounces Cotija cheese

Using a food processor fitted with the metal blade, mince the garlic and cilantro. Add about ⅓ of a fresh avocado, lemon juice, and Ranch dressing. Blend to combine. By hand, stir in minced sweet onion and adjust salt and pepper to taste. Refrigerate until ready to use. Dice remaining avocado and set aside.

Cut the lettuces into bite-size pieces.

Toss the lettuces, tomatoes, cheese, and about half the Cornfetti with 1 cup of the dressing. Garnish each salad with remaining Cornfetti and reserved avocado.

▼▼▼

Casa Rosa, *Dallas*   Yield: 4 cups

Jicama Salad

Casa Rosa serves this as a salad, but you can also use it as a salsa or relish to accompany enchilada plates or grilled fish and chicken. The fresh, light flavors are delicious with spicy foods and add a burst of color and flavor to traditional Tex-Mex plates.

The Dressing

¼	cup extra light olive oil	Whisk together the dressing ingredients and set aside.
½	cup fresh orange juice	
⅛	teaspoon garlic powder	
2	tablespoons fresh minced parsley	
½	teaspoon salt	
½	teaspoon white pepper	

2   scallions sliced, green and white parts

1   cup diced jicama, ¼-inch dice

1   cup diced red bell pepper, ¼-inch dice

½   cup diced poblano chile, roasted and peeled

1½ cups fresh corn, grilled, cut from the cob

Combine the green onion, jicama, red bell pepper, and poblano chile in a non-reactive mixing bowl. Brush whole corn cobs with oil and grill on all sides until lightly browned. Using a sharp knife, remove and separate corn kernels. Toss corn and dressing with jicama and peppers.

1   avocado, peeled, ¼-inch dice

Just prior to serving, gently mix in the avocado.

If serving as a salad, arrange the ingredients on mixed greens.

Mark Gonzales, Chef, *Dallas*   Yield: 6 servings

Radish-Cucumber Salad with Pumpkin Seeds and Goat Cheese

Mark suggests serving this for a summer luncheon with jalapeño cornbread or homemade soft corn tortillas.

The Vinaigrette

½ cup pumpkin seeds, salted and toasted (divided use)
¼ cup rice wine vinegar
1 tablespoon fresh lime juice
2 tablespoons fresh orange juice
1 clove garlic
2 teaspoons kosher salt
1 small poblano chile, roasted, seeded, and peeled
1 cup light olive oil
1 tablespoon fresh minced cilantro

To make the vinaigrette dressing, place ¼ cup pumpkin seeds in a blender and reserve the rest for garnish. Add vinegar, lime, and orange juice, garlic, salt, and poblano chile. Blend until well combined. Add the oil in a slow steady stream to emulsify the dressing. Add cilantro and set aside.

The Salad

1½ cups thinly sliced radishes
1½ cups chopped Roma tomatoes
1½ cups seeded, chopped cucumber
1 cup pitted calamata olives
1 cup julienne red onion
1 head Romaine lettuce, rinsed, chopped, and chilled
1 avocado, thinly sliced
8 ounces mild goat cheese, crumbled

Combine the vegetables and toss with about ¼ cup of the dressing.

Toss the chilled Romaine with another ⅓–¼ cup of the dressing. Divide the Romaine between six salad bowls. Mound the vegetables on top and garnish the salad with avocado slices and crumbled goat cheese. Drizzle each salad with about 1 tablespoon of the dressing and put more crumbled goat cheese on top.

▼▼

Mesa, Houston   Yield: 4 salads, 2 cups dressing

SOUTHWESTERN CAESAR SALAD

Blue Mesa offers contemporary Southwest cuisine in a warm, Santa Fe atmosphere. They opened with this colorful improvisation of the classic Caesar Salad. They prepare the salad tableside, as they do their fresh Guacamole. You could add grilled chicken or shrimp and make it an entrée salad.

Caesar Dressing

3	large cloves garlic
4	anchovies
3	large eggs
½	cup red wine vinegar
2	tablespoons Dijon mustard
¼	cup fresh cilantro, stemmed
2	serrano chiles, stemmed and seeded
½	teaspoon salt
½	teaspoon ground pepper

To make the dressing, combine garlic, anchovies, eggs, vinegar, mustard, cilantro, chiles, salt, and pepper in a blender or food processor and blend smooth.

1½	cups light olive oil
½	cup cotija cheese, freshly grated

With the blender running, slowly add the olive oil and blend until emulsified. Add cilantro and process a few seconds to blend in. Whip the cheese in by hand.

2	heads Romaine lettuce, cleaned
1	cup grilled or roasted corn kernels
1	cup red bell peppers roasted, peeled and diced
1	cup poblano chiles, roasted, peeled, and diced
1	cup Cotija cheese, grated
2	cups seasoned croutons

Cut the Romaine into bite-size pieces and put in a large bowl. Add the corn, peppers, chiles, cheese, and croutons. Toss to combine, then add the dressing and toss to lightly coat the greens.

Divided the salad among four plates. If adding chicken or shrimp, arrange cooked chilled shrimp or chicken atop the salad.

Garnish the salad with some Cotija cheese.

NOPALITO SALAD

The nopal cactus, also known as prickly pear, is sold in cans in many groceries. Mary Treviño calls this a very basic Mexican salad. You may use green peas or green beans if jicama is not available.

The Dressing

½ teaspoon salt or to taste
¼ teaspoon pepper
½ teaspoon dry mustard
¼ cup vinegar
½ cup oil
¼ teaspoon leaf oregano
½ cup sour cream

Whisk or blend the dressing ingredients vigorously to combine. Adjust seasonings to taste.

The Salad

1 small yellow onion, halved and cut in strips
1½ cups canned nopal cactus, chopped
1 3-ounce jar pimientos, rinsed, or 2 bell peppers, diced
2 cups jicama, chopped

Place the onions in a colander. Pour about 1 quart boiling water over them. This removes the raw taste and leaves the onions crisp. Rinse immediately with cold water and let stand.

Toss together the onions, cactus, pimientos or red bell peppers, and jicama. Toss the dressing and salad together just prior to serving.

Assembly and Presentation

1 cup sautéed chopped walnuts or pine nuts
  Boston lettuce leaves

Sauté the walnuts, if using, for 2 to 3 minutes, then drain on paper towels.

Place the salad on a lettuce leaf. Garnish with walnuts or pine nuts.

Z-Tejas, *Austin*   Yield: 2 servings

BLACKENED TUNA SALAD WITH CRISPY WALNUTS

You may substitute pumpkin seeds for the walnuts, but I urge you to try the walnuts. They are a little work, but delicious.

The Walnuts

2	cups chopped walnuts
1	tablespoon butter
2	tablespoons vegetable oil
1	teaspoon cayenne pepper
3	tablespoons packed brown sugar
¼	teaspoon salt

To prepare the walnuts, combine all the ingredients in a small mixing bowl. Heat a large skillet over low heat and cook, stirring often, until the sugar melts and coats the nuts. Transfer to a cookie sheet and bake at 325°, stirring several times, until the walnuts are crisp, about 25–30 minutes.

1	clove chopped garlic, minced
2	teaspoons honey
	juice of one lime
2	tablespoons balsamic vinegar
4	tablespoons light olive oil
	salt and pepper to taste

Whisk together the garlic, honey, lime juice, vinegar, and oil. Season with salt and pepper and set aside.

1	head red-tip leaf lettuce, rinsed
2	Roma tomatoes, cut in wedges
	light olive oil
2	4–6 ounce tuna steaks
	salt and pepper
2	tablespoons sesame seeds

Cut the lettuce into bite-size pieces and chill thoroughly.

Brush the tuna steaks with olive oil, season with salt and pepper. Coat with sesame seeds and sear in a hot nonstick or cast iron skillet. Cook about 2–2½ minutes on each side. Keep the tuna warm in a 300° oven while assembling the salads.

Toss lettuce and walnuts together with the vinaigrette. Mound on two dinner plates. Arrange tomato wedges around the edge of each plate. Cut the tuna into bite-size pieces and place in the center.

▼▼▼

Bennie Ferrell Catering, *Houston*   Yield: 12 servings

Sangría Mousse

This attractive dish may be used as a dessert or a salad—it is a delightful accompaniment to assertive entrées.

12 individual 1-cup molds or 1 angel food cake pan or bundt pan	Prepare the molds by rinsing them with cold water.

Clear Layer

2   tablespoons unflavored gelatin
1   cup cold water
¼   cup sugar
⅔   cup (1 6-ounce can) frozen lemonade concentrate
1   cup cold water
½   cup White Wine Sangría (see p. 15)
2   seedless oranges, peeled and sliced

Sprinkle gelatin over cold water and let stand 5 minutes to soften. Place over moderate heat and stir constantly until gelatin dissolves, about 5 minutes. Remove from heat.

Add sugar, stirring to dissolve, then frozen lemonade concentrate, stirring to melt. Add 1 cup cold water and Sangría, and then pour the mixture into each mold and chill until almost firm. Press orange slices into the mixture and refrigerate.

Cream Layer

3   tablespoons unflavored gelatin
1   cup cold water
½   cup sugar
1⅓   cups (1 12-ounce can) frozen lemonade concentrate
¾   cup cold water
1   cup White Wine Sangría (see p. 15)
1   cup heavy cream

Sprinkle gelatin over cold water and let stand 5 minutes to soften. Place over moderate heat and stir constantly until gelatin dissolves, about 5 minutes. Remove from heat.

Add sugar, stirring to dissolve, then frozen lemonade concentrate, stirring to melt. Add ¾ cup cold water and Sangría. Chill until mixture is the consistency of unbeaten egg white.

▼▼▼

Bennie Ferrell Catering

Whip heavy cream until stiff and then fold into the chilled mixture until very smooth. Pour over the chilled clear layer. Chill until firm.

Presentation

1   quart fresh strawberries, halved, or other fresh fruit

Unmold onto a serving platter and garnish with fresh strawberries or fresh fruit of your choice.

Storage, Freezing, and Advance Preparation

This may be made a day in advance and refrigerated, covered loosely, until ready to serve. Garnish at serving time.

▼▼

Mark Gonzales, Chef, *Dallas*   Yield: 6 cups

SMOKED CHICKEN SALAD

This recipe is a good example of how chipotle chiles can be used in nontraditional ways. It also illustrates how "contemporary Mexican" and "Southwest Cuisine" often travel the same path. This salad may be served on a bed of greens, rolled in a flour tortilla, or in a crisp, corn tortilla basket.

4–5	cups smoked chicken, diced (both white and dark meat)
3	stalks celery, sliced
1	red bell pepper, diced
½	cup red onion, diced
1–2	teaspoons salt
1	teaspoon coarsely ground black pepper
1	tablespoon Dijon mustard
1	tablespoon orange zest
1–1¼	cups Chipotle Ranch Dressing (p. 106)

To make the salad, combine all the ingredients and toss well to mix.

In a 3-quart saucepan, heat the oil to 350° over high heat. Allow the cut tortillas to stand at room temperature to "dry out" before frying.

6–8	corn tortillas, cut in julienne strips
	peanut oil

Fry the tortillas in several batches until crisp. Drain on paper towel and season lightly with salt.

1	head Romaine lettuce, shredded

Divide the lettuce between 6–8 large plates. Scatter a layer of tortilla strips on top of the lettuce. Place a scoop of the salad in the middle.

2	cups Roma tomatoes, diced
	fresh cilantro sprigs

Garnish each plate with diced tomatoes and a fresh cilantro sprig.

SHRIMP AND JICAMA SLAW WITH CHIPOTLE RANCH DRESSING

This crisp, colorful coleslaw is a nice accompaniment to crispy tacos or quesadillas. The smoky, spicy chipotle gives new life to ranch dressing. Increase the amount of chipotle for a spicier salad.

The Dressing

2	cups prepared ranch dressing
1	(canned) chipotle chile
1	tablespoon cilantro, minced
	pinch of salt
1	teaspoon fresh lime juice

To prepare the dressing, put the ingredients in a blender jar and blend until very smooth. Set aside.

The Salad

1	pound medium shrimp, cooked and deveined
1	cup julienne jicama, cut in julienne strips
2	cups red cabbage, thinly sliced
2	cups napa cabbage, thinly sliced
1	cup carrot, grated
½	cup each, red and green bell pepper, diced
1	teaspoon celery seed
⅓	cup toasted pine nuts, chopped

Slice the shrimp in half, lengthwise (through the vein). Combine the jicama, cabbage, shrimp, carrot, bell pepper, and celery seed in a medium-size bowl and toss to combine. Add about ¾ cups dressing and mix well.

Garnish each serving with toasted pine nuts.

POLLO SALAD

Bill Sadler and Chef Allan Mallett create new dishes from Mexican ingredients and offer many light dishes, artfully presented and perfectly prepared. This will remind you of a Cobb Salad. For best results, marinate the chicken 1–2 hours before grilling.

The Dressing

3 garlic cloves, peeled	Combine all the dressing ingredients
¼ cup fresh lemon juice	in a blender and blend smooth. If
½ teaspoon prepared mustard	quite thick, thin with a little cold
¾ cup light olive oil	water.
½ teaspoon salt	
⅛ teaspoon pepper	
1–2 tablespoons fresh grated Parmesan cheese	

1 small head Romaine lettuce, rinsed and chilled	Cut the lettuces into bite-size pieces and toss with carrots and dressing.
½ head iceberg lettuce, rinsed and chilled	Divide between 4 large plates. Arrange the remaining ingredients
1 large carrot, peeled and grated	on top, in rows.
5 Roma tomatoes, sliced	
5 boneless chicken breasts, grilled and diced	
4 ounces crumbled feta cheese	
5–6 tablespoons crumbled, crisp bacon	
¾ cup sliced black olives	
1 large avocado, diced	

KOKOPELLI

Left: Grilled Swordfish Taco with Cantelope Salsa (p. 150); Top: Puntas de Filet (p. 142);
Right: Blackened Chicken Puff Taco (p. 137); Salsa; Spinach con Queso (p. 62); *Bottom:*
Trout Tamale (p.185)

VEGETABLES AND ACCOMPANIMENTS

SAFFRON RICE
Kokopelli

SAUTÉED SQUASH
Author's Contribution

**ANCHO MASHED POTATOES WITH
SCALLIONS AND SOUR CREAM**
Mark Gonzales

AZTEC CORN
Author's Contribution

REFRIED BLACK BEANS
Blue Mesa

JULIA'S BEANS
Julia Segovia Ramírez

CORN PUDDING
Hudson's on the Bend

BLACK BEANS
Las Canarias

CORN CAKE
Blue Mesa

MEXICAN RICE
Author's Contribution

SAFFRON RICE

Kokopelli serves this colorful rice with their Las Escalopes and Pechuga Monterey. If you do not have saffron, you can use a small amount of tumeric or achiote powder to color the rice.

3	cups water or chicken broth
½	teaspoon saffron threads
1	teaspoon salt
1½	cups long grain white rice
2	tablespoons butter
1	clove garlic, minced
½	cup diced celery
½	cup diced carrots
¼	cup diced red bell pepper
¾	cup frozen peas
	salt and pepper to taste

In a medium saucepan, bring the water or chicken broth, saffron, and salt to a boil. Add the rice, lower the heat to a simmer, cover and cook without stirring for about 15 minutes.

Sauté the garlic, celery, carrot and red bell pepper in butter over medium heat for 3–4 minutes. Add the vegetables and peas to the cooked rice. Gently stir together and season to taste with salt and pepper.

▼▼

Author's Contribution Yield: 6–8 servings

SAUTÉED SQUASH

This is a colorful sauté that many restaurants use to accompany grilled chicken and fish entrées or as a light alternative to rice and beans on enchilada plates.

2	zucchini
2	yellow squash
1	green bell pepper, sliced
1	red bell pepper, sliced
1	small red or white onion, halved and thinly sliced
1–2	teaspoons vegetable or light olive oil
1	tablespoon butter
	salt and pepper
	fresh minced parsley

Cut the squashes lengthwise in half, then slice diagonally.

In a large skillet, heat the oil and butter over medium-high heat. Add the vegetables, peppers, and onions and stir-fry over medium heat until the onions are lightly browned and the squashes are tender-crisp.

Season with salt and pepper. Garnish the vegetables with fresh minced parsley.

Variation

The same vegetables may also be grilled. Slice squashes diagonally and cut the peppers in wide strips. Simply brush the squashes and peppers with oil and grill over a hot fire until marked on both sides and tender. Season with salt and pepper during grilling and serve with fresh lime wedges.

▼▼▼

Mark Gonzales, Chef, Dallas   Yield: 6–8 servings

Ancho Mashed Potatoes with Scallions and Sour Cream

It may seem unusual to find mashed potatoes in Mexican cooking, but it has been a tradition to use potatoes in both soft tacos and little masa turnovers for years. The combination of mashed potatoes topped with crisp tortilla chips is delicious.

8 cups russet potatoes, peeled and cut into large chunks	Put the potatoes in cold water to cover and bring to a boil.
	Cook potatoes in boiling water until tender, about 10–15 minutes.
¼ cup Ancho Chile Puree (p. 156) ¼ cup milk ⅓ cup sour cream 4 ounces Monterey Jack cheese, grated (optional)	While still hot, put the potatoes in a mixing bowl and add the Ancho Puree, milk, and sour cream. Whip until fluffy. (If adding cheese, add the cheese first to the hot potatoes, then add milk and sour cream.) Add more milk or sour cream, if necessary.
¼ cup sliced scallions 1 tablespoon salt (to taste) ½ teaspoon white pepper	Add seasonings and scallions and mix well.
	To serve, mound the potatoes on the plate and top with Cornfetti (p. 97) or 2–3 tortilla chips placed in the center.

AZTEC CORN

This is a great recipe for summer, when you are cooking outdoors. Your barbecue grill is also the perfect way to roast the peppers, giving them a wonderful flavor, but you may also cook Aztec Corn indoors.

3	large ears fresh sweet corn, in husks, white or yellow

Husk the corn, discarding silks and spotted husks. Soak the remaining husks for at least 30 minutes in water. Use as many husks as necessary to make 6 containers for about ¾ to 1 cup vegetables each. Then lay each one on a rectangular piece of aluminum foil, about 10 by 6 inches.

With a sharp knife, remove kernels from the cobs, taking care to use all the milky liquid.

3	tablespoons unsalted butter
6	green onions, sliced
¼	teaspoon salt
	pepper to taste
1	poblano chile, roasted, peeled, and chopped, or 1–2 canned green chiles, chopped
1	red bell pepper, chopped
1	cup chopped zucchini or peas (optional)

Melt the butter in a large skillet over medium heat. Add corn, green onions, salt, and pepper. Sauté about 5 minutes, and then add chopped chiles and red pepper. If using the optional vegetables, add to the skillet with the peppers.

½	cup salsa
	juice of 1 lime

Stir in salsa and lime juice, and taste and adjust seasonings.

Assembly and Presentation

6   fresh oregano or basil sprigs

Spoon about ¾ to 1 cup of the vegetables into the prepared husks, spreading them flat to make an oblong, boat-shaped container. Fold the foil over the husks, pinching the secure both ends and long edges. The vegetables will be grilled in this package.

Prepare barbecue grill. Arrange husks on cooler edge of grill. Grill about 8 to 10 minutes, without turning.

If baking in the oven, preheat to 375° and bake directly on the rack for 12 to 15 minutes.

To serve, open the foil and then slide the vegetables in their husks onto plates. Garnish with oregano or basil.

Author's Note

You may enclose the vegetables completely in the husks alone, securing in the same fashion as if making tamales. Brush with water while grilling to prevent the husks from scorching. This will impart more charcoal flavor.

Storage, Freezing, and Advance Preparation

The vegetables may be sautéed and the husks filled and sealed early in the day. Simply refrigerate until ready to grill.

REFRIED BLACK BEANS

Contemporary Mexican cooks have become quite conscious of the amount of fat used in cooking many traditional recipes, especially beans and rice. These have no fat at all, and quite a lot of flavor.

2–2½ cups black beans
5–6 cups water
2 chicken bouillon cubes
1 chipotle chile, including some of the liquid

2 cloves garlic, chopped
½ teaspoon ground cumin
½ teaspoon white pepper
1 14½-ounce can Mexican-style stewed tomatoes
1 onion, diced
1 stalk celery, diced
1 carrot, peeled and diced
salt to taste

Rinse the beans carefully and remove any stones. Put the beans, water, chicken cubes, and chipotle chile in a large saucepan or stock pot and bring to a boil.

Reduce the heat to medium-low and simmer 30 minutes. Add the garlic, seasonings, tomatoes, and vegetables. Simmer, uncovered, for 1½–2 hours or until the beans are soft. Cool for 15 minutes. Season to taste with salt.

Transfer the beans and all the vegetables to a food processor fitted with the metal blade. Use the pulse to chop, or run the machine to mash the beans, according to personal preference. Store beans refrigerated.

When ready to reheat, coat a skillet with a nonstick spray and place over medium heat. Add the beans and cook until hot. Adjust salt and pepper to taste.

▼▼

Julia Segovia Ramírez, *San Antonio* — Yield: 10 servings

JULIA'S BEANS

When Julia Segovia Ramírez moved to San Antonio in 1962, she brought with her the family traditions and recipes which had been handed down for generations. No cookbook from Texas would be complete without a recipe for beans. While the new trend is to move away from beans as an accompaniment to every dish, beans remain important, and Julia's are the best I have come across.

Julia's basic bean recipe is a staple, fairly bland dish that appears almost daily in most Mexican homes. For a spicier dish, Julia adds to the basic recipe to produce Beans a la Charra.

1	pound dried pinto beans
1	quart water

Soak the beans in about 1 quart hot water, just enough to thoroughly cover, for 30 minutes. Remove any hard pieces, and then rinse the beans in cool water and drain.

5–6	cups fresh water
1	teaspoon salt
2	cloves garlic, peeled
2–3	strips bacon, finely chopped (optional)

Cook the beans in 5–6 cups fresh water. After the first 30 minutes, add the salt, garlic, and bacon, if desired. Then let simmer 2 to 3 hours, watching carefully and adding water as needed. When fully cooked, adjust the salt to taste.

Variation Beans a la Charra

2	serrano chiles, stemmed, seeded, and minced
2	jalapeño chiles, stemmed, seeded, and minced
1	medium-size onion, chopped
10	strips bacon, chopped and sautéed until brown
2–3	tablespoons cilantro, minced

During the last 30 minutes, add all the ingredients except the cilantro. Stir in minced cilantro just before serving.

Julia Segovia Ramírez

Presentation

	snipped cilantro
4	ounces Monterey Jack cheese, grated
2–3	tomatoes, diced
1	onion, diced
	avocado slices
2–3	serrano chiles, diced

Serve with bowls of cilantro, cheese, tomatoes, onion, avocado, and chiles. Add homemade flour tortillas and you will have a good "vegetarian" buffet.

Storage, Freezing, and Advance Preparation

Beans always taste better if they are prepared in advance and reheated.

From Mariano Martínez Mariano's, Dallas

When storing pinto beans, drain off the excess liquid and refrigerate beans and liquid separately. The beans will stay fresh longer. You may add chicken stock when reheating.

▼▼▼

Hudson's on the Bend, *Austin*   Yield: 8–10 servings

CORN PUDDING

Jeff Blank says this is the most requested recipe from Hudson's on the Bend. The batter can be made a day ahead (another plus!) and baked later. You can serve this in crisp corn tortilla "cups," or tamale husks.

Dry mix

1¼	cups all-purpose flour
⅓	cup sugar
2½	tablespoons baking powder
½	teaspoon salt
½	teaspoon cayenne pepper

Preheat the oven to 350°.

Combine the dry ingredients in a small bowl and set aside.

Wet mix

6	whole eggs
½	cup whipping cream
¼	pound butter, melted
1	8-ounce can cream-style corn

In a larger bowl, whisk the eggs to a froth and add butter, cream, and creamed corn. Stir in dry ingredients and mix well.

Veggie mix

½	cup diced green bell pepper
½	cup diced red bell pepper
½	cup diced green chiles
1	cup fresh corn kernels

Fold in peppers, chiles, and corn kernels.

Butter a medium-size casserole dish and dust with flour. Add the batter and bake for 35–40 minutes or until golden brown and firm to the touch.

Note: If you have prepared the batter a day ahead, re-whisk the batter prior to transferring to a buttered baking dish.

▼▼▼

Las Canarias, *San Antonio*   Yield: 6–8 servings

BLACK BEANS

The Tomato Salsa

6 tomatoes, chopped
1 bunch cilantro, snipped
1 bunch scallions, thinly sliced
  salt and pepper to taste

No more than 3 to 4 hours before serving, combine tomatoes, cilantro, and scallions. Season to taste with salt and pepper and refrigerate.

The Mexican Cream

2 cups sour cream
1 cup heavy cream
1 teaspoon fresh lime juice

In a glass bowl, combine creams and lime juice and let stand at room temperature 2 hours. Refrigerate until ready to use.

The Beans

1½ cups dried black beans
10 strips bacon, chopped
2 carrots, roughly chopped
4 stalks celery, diced

1 quart water
6 cups chicken stock
1 onion, chopped
2 cloves garlic, minced
2 teaspoons salt
1/2 teaspoon pepper
1/2 teaspoon ground cloves

Wash and sort through the black beans. In a medium-size skillet, sauté the bacon until lightly browned. Add carrots and celery and cook an additional 2 to 3 minutes. Set aside.

In a large saucepan, combine the beans with water and chicken stock. Add the bacon mixture, onion, garlic, and seasonings and simmer over medium heat until the beans are tender, about 2 to 3 hours. Check and add more water if necessary to ensure a rich broth. Adjust the seasonings to taste.

Presentation

Serve the beans with the Mexican cream and tomato salsa. Rice may be served on the side.

Storage, Freezing, and Advance Preparation

Beans are best made ahead of time and reheated.

▼▼

Blue Mesa, *Dallas*   Yield: 8–10 servings

CORN CAKE

The corn cakes are made from a sweet tamale dough and come with many of the entrées at Blue Mesa and Mesa. The mixture is similar to a tamale filling, and may be steamed in tamale husks if you prefer. These are very popular at the restaurant and are sure to be a hit on a Mexican or Southwest buffet. You may use frozen (thawed) corn, canned corn, or fresh corn in season.

4 tablespoons vegetable shortening 8 tablespoons butter or margarine 1 whole egg	Place the shortening and butter in a mixer or food processor and whip until the mixture becomes light and creamy, about 5–8 minutes. Add the egg to aid blending.
1½ cups corn kernels	In a blender, grind the corn coarsley. Do not puree. Set aside.
1 cup masa harina 1 cup warm water	Combine the masa and water in a small bowl, stirring well. Add to the shortening and butter and mix until light and fluffy.
¼ cup cornmeal ½ cup sugar ⅓ cup whipping cream 2 teaspoons baking powder ½ teaspoon salt	Add corn, cornmeal, sugar, whipping cream, baking powder, and salt to the masa and mix well.

Blue Mesa

Pour the mixture into a 1½-quart bowl, cover and place in a larger bowl half filled with hot water. "Tent" the foil over the bowl to prevent it from sticking to the top of the mixture. Bake at 375° for about 1½ hours, or until firm. Let stand in the hot water 10–15 minutes before serving. Use an ice cream scoop to make a "cake" shape for service.

Variation

You may bake these in 8-ounce molds. In this case, the baking time will be reduced to about 30 minutes.

▼▼

Author's Contribution   Yield: 5–6 servings

MEXICAN RICE

Rice is a standard accompaniment to many Mexican dishes, whether contemporary or Tex-Mex. This is a basic recipe with several variations. Contemporary chefs still prepare rice, but enhance the rice with vegetables, other types of rice . . . even grains.

2	tablespoons corn oil
1	cup onion, diced

In a large skillet, heat the oil over medium heat. Add the onion and sauté until wilted.

1–16	ounce can diced tomatoes, including juices
1½	cups cooked corn
1	cup cooked green peas
1	cup cooked diced carrots
½–1	teaspoon salt
½	teaspoon garlic powder

Stir in tomatoes and bring to a simmer. Add corn, peas, carrots, and seasonings and set aside.

2	tablespoons corn oil
1	cup long grain white rice
2	cups chicken broth

In a 2-quart saucepan, heat the oil over medium heat. Add the rice and sauté about 5 minutes or until the rice turns white. Add the chicken broth and bring to a boil. Cover and simmer over low heat for about 15 minutes. Check after 8–10 minutes and add additional broth if necessary. Stir in the vegetables, cover and let stand about 10 minutes, or until all the liquid is absorbed and vegetables are heated. Stir in fresh minced cilantro.

Presentation

minced cilantro

▼▼▼

Author's Contribution

Variations

1) In place of the carrots and peas, add 2 red bell peppers and 2 chile poblanos, roasted, peeled, and diced.

2) Omit the tomatoes and increase the chicken broth to 3 cups. Use ½ cup wild rice and ½ cup brown rice in place of white rice. Garnish the finished rice with ½ cup toasted pine nuts or pecans (chopped).

3) Replace the canned tomatoes with an equal amount of fresh, pureed tomatillos. Omit all vegetables except the corn and onions. In this case, add at least ¼ cup each minced cilantro and parsley just before serving, to enhance the color.

Casa Rosa

Bottom: Goat Cheese Relleno (p. 179); *Left:* Wild Mushroom and Goat Cheese Enchilada (p. 140); *Top:* Chicken Poblano Chowder (p. 90); *Salsa; Right:* Red Snapper Fajita (p. 207)

TORTILLA SPECIALTIES

MEXICAN PIZZA
La Esquina

QUESADILLA AZTECA
Author's Contribution

BLUE CRAB ENCHILADAS
Mesa

WILD MUSHROOM ENCHILADAS
Z-Tejas

CHICKEN AND MUSHROOM ENCHILADAS
Blue Mesa

GORDITAS
Cappy's

CHICKEN CHILAQUILES
La Hacienda

BLACKENED CHICKEN PUFF TACOS
Kokopelli

SOFT CHICKEN TACOS
La Fogata

WILD MUSHROOM AND GOAT CHEESE
ENCHILADAS
Casa Rosa

GREEN CHICKEN ENCHILADAS
La Fogata

PUNTA'S DE FILETE
Kokopelli

SHRIMP ENCHILADAS
Casa Rosa

FISH TACOS
Mark Gonzales

NINFA'S CRAB ENCHILADAS
Ninfa's

SAN MIGUEL'S CRABMEAT ENCHILADAS
Fonda San Miguel

GRILLED SWORDFISH TACOS
Kokopelli

SQUASH ENCHILADAS
Via Real

▼▼

La Esquina, *Dallas*   Yield: Varies according to use

MEXICAN PIZZA

This delicious layered concoction, the invention of the chefs at the Anatole, is served for Saturday brunch. It is a most colorful and satisfying dish, which may be an appetizer for 16 to 18, a brunch or lunch entrée for 12, or dinner for 6 hungry teenagers. It holds well on a warming tray and makes a spectacular buffet dish.

1 pound ground beef	In a large skillet, sauté the ground meat 5 to 8 minutes until fully cooked. Drain off all excess fat.
2 tomatoes, diced 1 onion, chopped 1 teaspoon ground cumin 1–2 teaspoons chile powder ½ teaspoon salt ¼ teaspoon pepper 1½ cups Julia's Beans (see p. 116), partially mashed	Add the tomatoes and onion to the meat and cook 3 to 5 minutes more until the onion is soft. Season the beef mixture with cumin, chile powder, salt, and pepper to taste. Stir the beans into the mixture and set aside.
1½–2 cups shredded cooked chicken (optional) 1 cup picante sauce (optional)	Mix the cooked chicken with the picante sauce, if using.
1¼ pounds longhorn cheddar cheese, shredded 1¼ pounds Monterey Jack cheese, shredded	Divide the cheese into thirds.
2 red peppers 4 green peppers 4 jalapeño chiles, seeded 3 tomatoes	Chop the vegetables and set them aside.

▼▼▼

La Esquina   Yield: 2 servings

Assembly and Presentation

| 14 | 12-inch burrito-size flour tortillas |
| 2 | cups sour cream butter |

Use a buttered jelly roll pan with sides. Begin with 6 tortillas, covering the entire surface and overlapping the sides. Next, spread all the ground beef and bean mixture, topped with half the sour cream. Sprinkle with both the cheeses, using $\frac{1}{3}$ the total amount. Scatter $\frac{1}{3}$ of the chopped peppers and tomatoes over the cheeses. Repeat, using only 4 tortillas for the second layer. Spread with the chicken (if using), followed by the remaining sour cream, $\frac{1}{3}$ of the cheeses, and $\frac{1}{3}$ of the vegetables. Repeat, using the final 4 tortillas. Press the sides of the tortillas inward all around the edge of the pan to enclose filling. Top with remaining cheeses and chopped tomatoes and peppers. Brush all exposed tortilla surfaces with butter. Bake at 350° about 35 to 45 minutes.

fresh parsley

Sprinkle with fresh parsley just before serving. Cut into squares to serve.

Storage, Freezing, and Advance Preparation

The pizza may be assembled 24 hours in advance and refrigerated until ready to bake. It may be frozen for 2 to 3 months; thaw before baking.

QUESADILLA AZTECA

This is similar to a stacked enchilada. It's a good dish for entertaining because it can be prepared in advance and presented as an individual serving.

15	corn tortillas
	corn oil

Heat the oil to warm in a small skillet. Dip each tortilla briefly to soften. Drain on paper towels.

	Enchilada Sauce (p. 34)
	Corn and Black Bean Relish (p. 28)
12–14	ounces Spicy Jack Cheese, grated
6	cups diced smoked turkey or grilled chicken

On a large cookie sheet, assemble the quesadilla as follows: dip 5 tortillas in the Enchilada Sauce to make a base for the quesadillas. Top each one with about ⅓ cup of the Corn and Black Bean Relish, followed by 1½ ounces of cheese and 1 to 1¼ cups of diced turkey. Repeat, making another layer of tortillas and filling. Top with a third tortilla, dipped in sauce. Cover loosely with foil and bake in a 350°oven until hot, about 15–20 minutes.

Keep remaining Enchilada Sauce hot.

3	cups Pico de Gallo (p. 24)
	Cornfetti (p. 97)
	Mexican Cream (p. 119)

To serve, use a large spatula and transfer quesadillas to five dinner plates. Ladle with additional sauce and top with decorative drizzles of Mexican Cream. Top with a handful of Cornfetti and place three mounds of Pico de Gallo around the base.

▼▼

Mesa, *Houston*   Yield: 6 servings

BLUE CRAB ENCHILADAS

The Veracruzana Sauce for these enchiladas may be used to prepare Red Snapper Veracruz or as a sauce for almost any grilled or sautéed fish or shellfish. Mesa serves these with their signature corncake which makes a light entrée.

The Filling

2	tablespoons olive oil
2	tablespoons butter
1	clove garlic, minced
¾	cups diced onion
1	tablespoon diced (canned) jalapeños
3	tablespoons juice from the can
3	cups diced tomatoes
1	tablespoon minced parsley
2	tablespoons minced cilantro
½	teaspoon salt
¼	teaspoon black pepper
1	pound fresh crabmeat

Heat the oil and butter in a skillet over medium heat. Add the garlic and onion and sauté until translucent. Stir in all the ingredients except the crab meat and continue to sauté, stirring often, for about 10 minutes. Add the crabmeat and cook, tossing gently to incorporate, for 3–4 minutes.

The Sauce

3	ounces light olive oil
2	cloves garlic, minced
1	cup diced onions
4	Roma tomatoes, peeled and diced
3	ounces green olives, sliced
2	tablespoons capers
2	bay leaves
¼	teaspoon each, thyme, marjoram salt and pepper
½	cup chicken broth
2	14.5-ounce cans diced tomatoes

To make the sauce, heat the salad oil in a saucepan and sauté garlic and onion until lightly browned, about 5 minutes. Add the tomatoes, green olives, capers, bay leaves, and seasonings and cook for about 4–5 minutes, being careful not to burn. Stir in the chicken broth and tomatoes and simmer for about 25 minutes. Discard bay leaves.

Mesa

12 corn tortillas	One at a time, dip the tortillas in hot oil to soften and seal. Drain on paper towels. Spoon about 1½–2 ounces of the filling in each one, roll and place seam side down in a casserole dish. Spoon a small amount of sauce over the tortillas. Cover and heat in a 350° oven for about 15 minutes. (If prepared in advance, and enchiladas are quite cold, double the heating time.)
6–8 ounces Cotija cheese minced parsley	Sprinkle each serving with Cotija cheese and minced parsley.

Z-Tejas, *Austin*   Yield: 4 servings

WILD MUSHROOM ENCHILADAS

Wild mushrooms are a favorite filling for enchiladas and there are as many versions as there are chefs. This filling is equally good for a soft taco or griddled quesadilla made with flour tortillas.

Ancho Chile Sauce

2	ancho chiles
	water
2½	cups whipping cream
2	tablespoons honey
	salt and pepper to taste

To make the sauce, rinse ancho chiles and remove seeds and stems. Toast chiles in a 300° oven for 3–4 minutes. Put the chiles in a saucepan with enough water to cover. Bring to a boil and simmer for 8–10 minutes. Let stand until soft. Drain, discard water, and blend the chiles to puree. Meanwhile bring the cream to a boil and boil until reduced by about half, for 10–12 minutes. Stir in honey and ancho pureeadding water if needed to aid blending. Season to taste with salt and pepper.

2	cups sliced mushrooms, shitake, oyster, and portobello
2	tablespoons butter
¼	cup chopped onion
2	tomatoes, chopped
2	tablespoons minced cilantro
1	medium-ripe avocado, diced

Sauté the mushrooms and onion in hot butter over medium heat for 3–4 minutes. Add tomato, cilantro, and avocado and cook about 1 minute to heat and combine.

| ½ | cup vegetable oil |
| 8 | corn tortillas |

Heat the oil in a medium skillet and dip tortillas one at a time to soften and seal. Drain excess oil.

| ¾ | cup Cotija cheese, crumbled |

Fill each tortilla with mushroom filling. Use about half the cheese and crumble on top. Drizzle with a small amount of sauce and roll up. Place seam side down in a baking dish and top with remaining sauce and crumbled cheese.

Bake in a 400° oven for 10–15 minutes, or until hot.

Blue Mesa, *Dallas*   Yield: 6 servings

CHICKEN AND MUSHROOM ENCHILADAS

This recipe was developed in response to customer interest in "light" Mexican dishes. It quickly became one of the most popular items at Blue Mesa.

Salsa de Tomatillo (p. 42)

1	onion, diced
2	poblano peppers, roasted, peeled and diced
1	red bell pepper, diced
1	tablespoon minced garlic
1	pound fresh mushrooms, sliced
2	ounces white wine
3	ounces chicken broth
½	pound fresh spinach, chopped
	salt and pepper to taste
1	pound Fajita chicken, diced (p. 204)

12   corn tortillas

Prepare the Tomatillo Sauce and set aside.

Spray a large skillet with a vegetable coating spray. Add the onion, peppers, garlic, and mushrooms and toss briefly. Add the wine and chicken broth and simmer the vegetables until the onions are translucent. Add the spinach and cook over low heat until wilted and most of the liquid has evaporated. Season to taste with salt and pepper. Combine the spinach mixture with cooked chicken.

Soften the tortillas in a microwave, wrapped in plastic wrap, 3 or 4 at a time. Dip tortillas, one at a time, in warm Tomatillo Sauce, fill with about ½ cup of the filling, roll up and place seam side down in a casserole dish. Spoon additional sauce over the enchiladas. Cover and place in a 350° oven to warm for about 15 minutes.

Garnish and Presentation

crumbled Feta cheese
fresh cilantro sprig

Serve 2 enchiladas per person with additional sauce and a small amount of crumbled Feta cheese. Serve with Refried Black Beans (p. 115).

Cappy's, *San Antonio*

Yield: 1 dozen Gorditas

GORDITAS

Gorditas are fat little tortillas made from fresh corn masa, then fried and split to hold various fillings. Cappy makes the masa into little cups, a more attractive and practical approach.

The Filling

3–4	cups Picadillo (see p. 171)
1½	cups Guacamole (see p. 32)
1	head lettuce, shredded
3	tomatoes, diced
12	ounces cheddar cheese, grated

Have the Picadillo and the Guacamole ready. Have the lettuce shredded, the tomatoes diced, and the cheese grated. Refrigerate.

The Masa Cups

fresh corn masa (1–2 ounces per mold) See note p. 134
peanut oil for frying

Spray 3-inch tin molds with a non-stick vegetable coating. Press masa into each mold, and, using tongs, deep-fry in hot oil at 375°. The molds will sink to the bottom and the masa will soon separate from the molds. Turn to lightly brown on both sides, about 2 minutes. Take care not to overcook or the shells will be tough.

Assembly and Presentation

sour cream

Place about ¼ to ⅓ cup Picadillo in each masa cup. Top with 1 ounce of cheddar cheese in each shell. Top this with shredded lettuce, Guacamole, diced tomatoes, and sour cream. Serve immediately.

Cappy's

Author's Note

If fresh masa is not available, use masa harina, prepared according to the package directions. Tin molds can be found in most specialty shops.

Storage, Freezing, and Advance Preparation

The Picadillo may be prepared several days ahead. The lettuce, tomatoes, and cheese may be prepared 3 hours ahead. However, for best results, fry the masa cups just prior to serving.

▼▼

La Hacienda, *San Antonio*   Yield: 8–10 servings

CHICKEN CHILAQUILES

Chilaquiles must have originated in an effort to use stale corn tortillas; however, the delicious dish is well worth creating, even if you have to buy fresh tortillas and toast them. Use a buttered 9-by-12-inch casserole dish or a standard loaf pan. When preparing the ingredients, keep in mind that the amounts are flexible.

2	onions, chopped	In a medium-size skillet, sauté the onions and garlic in bacon fat until soft and translucent, about 5 to 8 minutes.
1	clove garlic, minced	
2–3	tablespoons bacon fat	

2	1-pound cans tomatoes, coarsely chopped, including juice	Stir the tomatoes and their juice into the onions. Season to taste with salt, pepper, and chile powder.
1	13-ounce can Rotel tomatoes and chiles	
1	teaspoon salt or to taste	
½	teaspoon black pepper	
½–1	teaspoon chile powder	

1	dozen tortillas	Cut the tortillas in half and then toast in a preheated 350° oven for about 8 minutes.

Assembly and Presentation

2	cups cooked chicken, cut in bite-size pieces	To assemble the chilaquiles, make 2 or 3 layers of tortillas, sauce, chicken, and cheese, ending with the cheese on top. Bake in a preheated 350° oven for about 30 minutes. During the last 5 minutes of cooking time, spread with a moderately thick layer of sour cream. If using a loaf pan, increase the cooking time by about 8 minutes.
10–12	ounces Monterey Jack cheese, grated	
1–1½	cups sour cream	

▼▼

La Hacienda

minced fresh parsley or
cilantro

Garnish with parsley or cilantro when serving. Accompany with a fresh steamed vegetable or a fruit salad.

Storage, Freezing, and Advance Preparation

You may prepare this casserole 12 hours in advance or the day before, refrigerating overnight. It will freeze quite well; thaw completely before baking.

▼▼

Kokopelli, *Dallas*   Yield: 8 servings

BLACKENED CHICKEN PUFF TACOS

Puff tacos are made from fresh, uncooked corn tortillas or specially prepared (baked) tortillas. In order to make these at home, you need to start with masa harina and make fresh tortillas, then fry them in hot oil, spooning oil on top of the flat tortilla to encourage puffing. You might opt to purchase a few puff taco shells from your favorite restaurant when making this dish at home, or simply use a traditionally shaped taco shell.

	olive oil
1	16-ounce can refried pinto beans
	milk (if needed)
	salt and pepper

Heat 1–2 tablespoons olive oil in a medium sauté pan over medium heat. Add the beans and "mash" flat. When they are slightly crusty, stir in salt and pepper to taste. Add 3–4 tablespoons of milk, if the beans are too thick. Set aside and keep warm.

4	6-ounce chicken breasts, skinless, boneless
2	tablespoons cajun seasoning
3–4	tablespoons vegetable oil

Coat the chicken breasts with cajun seasoning. Grill or sauté the chicken in hot oil, over medium heat on both sides, for about 3–4 minutes.

If grilling, coat the chicken breasts first with oil, then cajun seasonings. When "blackened," remove from heat and finish cooking in a 350° oven 4–5 minutes. Dice the chicken in small cubes.

½	cup sun dried tomatoes (packed in oil)
¾	cup Queso (p. 62)
4–5	cups thinly sliced iceberg lettuce
½	cup light sour cream
1	cup diced Roma tomatoes
	Chile Árbol Sauce (p. 43)

To assemble each taco, break open the top to make a small opening. Spoon 3–4 tablespoons of beans in each shell. Drain all oil from the tomatoes, coarsely chop, and place atop the beans. Top with a large spoonful of Queso (without the spinach), shredded lettuce, and diced chicken. Garnish with a handful of lettuce and diced tomatoes. Drizzle with sour cream.

Serve Chile Árbol Sauce on the side.

La Fogata, *San Antonio*   Yield: 5 servings, 2 per person, 4 cups sauce

SOFT CHICKEN TACOS

This light and low-calorie sauce is my favorite at La Fogata; it is also served over huevos rancheros. These chicken tacos are a unique item at La Fogata.

½   onion, cut in thin strips
1   bell pepper, cut in thin strips
2   tablespoons vegetable oil
1½   tablespoons flour

In a large skillet, sauté the onion and pepper in 2 tablespoons hot oil until the onions are soft and translucent, 5 to 8 minutes. Sprinkle with flour, stirring constantly.

½   the tomatoes from a 14½–16-ounce can Italian-style tomatoes, including all the juice

Roughly chop the tomatoes and stir both tomatoes and their juices into the onion-and-pepper mixture.

1   4-ounce can tomato sauce
2   tablespoons pimiento, diced
¼   teaspoon garlic powder
½   teaspoon salt
¼   teaspoon pepper
3¼   cups chicken stock

Add tomato sauce, pimiento, seasonings, and chicken stock, and cook about 7 minutes. Reduce heat and simmer 20 to 30 minutes. The sauce may cook slowly for an additional 30 to 45 minutes, thus reducing and thickening without adding flour, or add flour as follows.

In a small measure, stir 1½ tablespoons flour into about 1 cup of the sauce to make a smooth paste. Then add this mixture to the sauce and cook an additional 5 to 10 minutes, or until the flour is cooked and the sauce thickened. Adjust seasonings.

3   chicken breasts (singles)

Simmer the chicken, in enough water to cover, about 20 minutes or until cooked but still tender. Remove skin and bones and then shred the meat in small pieces.

▼▼▼

La Fogata

| | vegetable oil | In a medium-size skillet, heat oil to about 300°. Pass tortillas into hot oil for a few seconds to soften and seal. Remove carefully and set aside between paper towels. Do this just prior to assembly. |
| 10 | corn tortillas | |

Assembly and Presentation

Dip the tortillas in the sauce and then fill with the shredded chicken, moistened with a small amount of the sauce. Roll up and place seam side down in a casserole dish. Bake, covered, to heat, about 10 to 12 minutes. Top with additional sauce when serving.

Storage, Freezing, and Advance Preparation

The sauce may be made several days in advance; however, these soft tacos are best when made with freshly cooked and shredded chicken. While you may make them ahead and then reheat, you will lose some of the quality that makes this dish so special.

Casa Rosa, *Dallas*   Yield: 4 servings

WILD MUSHROOM AND GOAT CHEESE ENCHILADAS

If blue corn tortillas are difficult to obtain, use yellow or white corn. Goat cheese has become as popular with Mexican chefs as with "new" American chefs and you'll "taste" why when you try this dish.

3	tablespoons butter or margarine
¾	pound domestic mushrooms, stemmed and sliced
½	pound shitake mushrooms, sliced
½	cup diced onion
	pinch of ground sage
2	teaspoons seasoning salt
2–3	drops mesquite flavoring or Worcestershire sauce

Heat the butter or margarine over medium heat in a large skillet. Add mushrooms and onions and sauté a few minutes until softened. Add seasonings and continue to cook until most of the liquid has evaporated.

10	ounces mild goat cheese, at room temperature
¼	cup Pico de Gallo (p. 24)
8	corn tortillas, preferably thin vegetable oil

Combine the goat cheese and Pico de Gallo and set aside.

Heat about 1–1½ cups of vegetable oil in a medium skillet over medium heat and dip the tortillas, one at a time, to soften. Lay tortillas flat and put about 1½ ounces each of the goat cheese and mushroom mixture on each one. Roll up and place seam side down in a baking dish.

	Chile Cascabel Sauce (p. 39)
4	ounces grated Monterey Jack cheese

Ladle about 2–2½ cups sauce on top and bake, covered, in a 350° oven for about 20–25 minutes, or until hot. Uncover and top with Monterey Jack cheese and return to the oven to melt the cheese.

½	cup diced Roma tomatoes
	fresh minced parsley
	Jicama Salad (p. 98)

Serve 2 enchiladas per person and garnish each serving with diced tomatoes and fresh minced parsley.

▼▼

La Fogata, *San Antonio*   Yield: 4 servings, 2 per person

Green Chicken Enchiladas

Green enchiladas are almost a staple in parts of Texas, but the secret in this recipe is Carmen Calvillo's green sauce. Customers always request her recipe—it's the cilantro that makes it distinct.

1¼ pound tomatillos, quartered	Boil the tomatillos in ½ cup water with garlic, chiles, and salt and pepper until soft, about 15 to 20 minutes.
½ cup water	
1 clove garlic, whole	
2 serrano chiles	
¼ teaspoon salt	Puree the cooked sauce in a blender to liquefy. While blending, add washed cilantro leaves. Set aside. The sauce yield is about 2½ cups. It will thicken upon standing, and you may need to thin with chicken stock.
¼ teaspoon pepper	
⅓ cup cilantro leaves, loosely packed, chopped	
chicken stock, if needed	

1¼ pound tomatillos, quartered
½ cup water
1 clove garlic, whole
2 serrano chiles
¼ teaspoon salt
¼ teaspoon pepper
⅓ cup cilantro leaves, loosely packed, chopped
chicken stock, if needed

Boil the tomatillos in ½ cup water with garlic, chiles, and salt and pepper until soft, about 15 to 20 minutes.

Puree the cooked sauce in a blender to liquefy. While blending, add washed cilantro leaves. Set aside. The sauce yield is about 2½ cups. It will thicken upon standing, and you may need to thin with chicken stock.

2 whole chicken breasts
salt
1 cup chicken stock

Simmer the chicken in lightly salted water until tender, about 10 to 15 minutes. (Chicken will be slightly undercooked.) Bone and shred the cooked chicken and then, just prior to serving, reheat in 1 cup chicken stock. This will heat the chicken without overcooking.

1 cup peanut oil
8 corn tortillas

In a medium-size skillet, heat oil to about 300°. Pass tortillas into hot oil for a few seconds to soften and seal. Remove carefully and set aside between paper towels. Do this just prior to assembly.

Assembly and Presentation

1 cup sour cream
1 pound mozzarella cheese, grated

Fill softened tortillas with shredded chicken and 1–2 tablespoons of the sauce. Roll up and place seam side down in a casserole. Pour the green sauce over the top, and garnish with sour cream and cheese. Place in a hot oven 5 to 8 minutes or just long enough to melt the cheese.

▼▼

Kokopelli, *Dallas*   Yield: 4 servings

Punta's De Filete

This hearty meat sauce was created by Kokopelli's executive chef. I have substituted a Knorr Swiss product for the sauce preparation since most home cooks do not have veal stock on hand. The result lacks the distinctive rich taste of the veal stock, but is similar and was a favorite among taste-testers.

The Sauce

3	strips bacon, diced
1	carrot, diced
1	small onion, diced
1	celery stalk, diced
1	serrano chile, minced
2	garlic cloves, minced
1	Roma tomato diced
1	package Knorr Swiss Demi Glace (brown sauce)
1½–2	cups water
1	bunch cilantro stems
	salt and pepper to taste
2	pounds beef tenderloin trimmed and cubed
4	ounces olive oil
	The Sauce (see above)
2	ounces butter
	Black Beans (p. 119)
4	corn tostada shells
	Cornfetti (p. 97)
12	cilantro sprigs

To make the sauce, sauté the bacon in a saucepan until it begins to get crisp. Add the carrot, onion, celery, serrano, garlic and tomato and cook on low heat until the vegetables are a medium-brown color, about 6–8 minutes.

Stir the demi-glace powder and water together until smooth. Slowly add the mixture to the vegetables and stir until thickened and smooth. Add cilantro and cook a few more minutes. Season to taste with salt and pepper. Stir in the butter. Strain and reserve.

Sear the tenderloin in olive oil for 3–4 minutes, or until juices no longer run red. Stir in the reserved sauce and butter.

Spoon the Black Beans on 4 serving plates and top with a corn tostada. Mound the beef on top and garnish with Cornfetti strips and fresh cilantro sprigs.

▼▼

Casa Rosa, *Dallas*   Yield: 4 servings

SHRIMP ENCHILADAS

Shrimp, goat cheese, and Pico de Gallo make an interesting combination for enchiladas that go well with a variety of sauces. Choose from a Green Chile Sauce, Tomatillo Sauce, or Cascabel Sauce. Casa Rosa serves these in blue corn tortillas, often difficult to find in most stores, so feel free to substitute your favorite brand of corn tortilla.

10	ounces mild goat cheese, at room temperature
⅓	cup Pico de Gallo (p. 24)
2	tablespoons butter
	salt and pepper
1	pound fresh shrimp, peeled and deviened
½	cup diced onion
⅓	cup chopped cilantro
1	cup vegetable oil
8	blue corn tortillas
	Chile Cascabel Sauce (p. 39)

Mash the goat cheese with a fork to soften and gently mix in the Pico de Gallo. Set aside.

Melt the butter over medium heat in a large skillet. Add the shrimp and sauté until pink, about 2–3 minutes. Season with salt and pepper. Set 4 whole shrimp aside for garnish and coarsely chop the rest. Combine with onion and cilantro and set aside.

Heat the oil in a skillet. One at a time, dip the tortillas to soften and seal. Drain on paper towels to absorb excess oil. Put about 1½ ounces goat cheese on each tortilla and top with chopped shrimp. Roll enchiladas and place seam side down in a baking dish. Ladle 2–3 tablespoons Cascabel Sauce over the enchiladas, cover with foil and place in a preheated 350° oven to warm, about 12–15 minutes.

5–6	ounces grated Monterey Jack cheese
½	cup diced Roma tomatoes
	fresh minced parsley
	Jicama Salad (p. 98)

Serve 2 enchiladas per person, topped with additional heated sauce. Garnish each serving with a whole shrimp, grated cheese, diced tomatoes, and fresh minced parsley. Serve with Jicama Salad.

Mark Gonzales, Chef, *Dallas*   Yield: 10–12 tacos

FISH TACOS

These ancho-glazed fish tacos may be served with any of the salsas or relishes in this book as well as the Roasted Garlic and White Bean Dip and Radish Salad that Mark suggests. These are "soft" tacos, but you may also use crisp taco shells.

The Radish Salad

1	pound red radishes, thinly sliced
2	tablespoons chopped cilantro
2	tablespoons fresh lime juice
2	tablespoons fresh orange juice
2	tablespoons light olive oil
1	tablespoon coarse salt
1	serrano chile, seeded and diced
2	teaspoons Tabasco sauce

To make the Radish Salad, toss all of the ingredients together and let chill for one hour.

The Ancho-Honey Glaze

2	ancho chiles, toasted, seeded, stemmed, and diced
1–1½	cups water
6	Roma tomatoes, halved
1	tablespoon tamari sauce (light soy sauce)
1	cup honey
2	teaspoons Tabasco sauce
2	teaspoons fresh lime juice

For the glaze, simmer the ancho chiles in water until they are soft and make a paste. (Watch carefully so the water does not boil away).

Meanwhile, sprinkle the tomatoes with salt and roast skin side up in a 400° oven until skins can be easily removed and the tomatoes are soft, about 10–15 minutes. Remove and discard skins.

Mark Gonzales

Put chili paste, tomatoes, tamari, and honey in a medium saucepan over high heat and bring to a boil. Reduce to a simmer and cook to a glaze consistency, about 15–20 minutes. Add Tabasco and lime juice and set aside.

The Fish

2	pounds mahi, swordfish, or red snapper cut into 4-ounce portions
2	tablespoons olive oil
2	cloves garlic, minced
1	tablespoon orange zest
1	tablespoon coarse salt
16	scallions, trimmed
2	cups finely sliced Napa cabbage
	Corn Tortillas, warmed until soft
	Roasted Garlic and White Bean Dip (p. 33)

To prepare the fish, combine the olive oil, garlic, orange zest, and salt and spread over the fish. Cover and refrigerate for one hour.

Grill the fish over a hot charcoal or gas-fired grill for about 3 minutes per side. Brush liberally with the ancho glaze during grilling. Grill the scallions at the same time until lightly marked. Remove. "Flake" the fish and chop the scallions.

To assemble the tacos, spread warm corn tortillas with the Roasted Garlic and White Bean Dip and top with flaked fish, thinly sliced cabbage, chopped scallions, and Radish Salad.

▼▼

Ninfa's, Houston   Yield: 6 servings, 2 per person, 4 cups sauce

NINFA'S CRAB ENCHILADAS

This is Ninfa's special version—a delightfully delicate dish when made with thin corn tortillas. I have taken the liberty of soaking the enchiladas in cream, which makes an even lighter dish, almost reminiscent of crepes.

1	medium-size white onion, chopped
3	large tomatoes, peeled and chopped
1	jalapeño chile, stemmed, seeded, and minced
½	stick butter
½	teaspoon salt or to taste
¼	teaspoon white pepper

In a medium-size skillet, sauté the onion, tomatoes, and chile in butter for about 8 minutes. Add seasonings, then remove and set aside.

1	pound fresh or thawed frozen crabmeat
3–4	tablespoons butter

In the same skillet, sauté the crabmeat in butter several minutes or just long enough to heat through. Stir in half the reserved sauce and set aside.

½–¾	cup safflower oil or clarified butter
12	thin corn tortillas

In a medium-size skillet, heat the oil or butter to about 300°. Dip each tortilla in the oil or butter briefly to soften and seal, about 10 seconds, then press between paper towels to drain.

Assembly and Presentation

1	cup light cream

Divide the filling between the tortillas, then fold and place seam side down in a buttered 8½-by-11-inch baking dish. Pour the cream over the tortillas and then cover and let soak for 1 hour at room temperature or 3 to 4 hours refrigerated.

146

Ninfa's

2 cups (about 8 ounces) Monterey Jack cheese, grated

Spoon the remaining sauce over the soaked enchiladas, then top with grated cheese and bake in a preheated 375° oven for about 10 to 15 minutes or until heated through.

fresh cilantro or watercress

Garnish with fresh cilantro or watercress.

Serve with wedges of seasonal fruits, such as melon or papaya, or a spinach-stuffed tomato, or a spinach soufflé.

Storage, Freezing, and Advance Preparation

You may make the enchiladas early in the day, allowing them to soak in the cream. Prepare the sauce also, refrigerating until ready to bake. These enchiladas also may be frozen, providing the crab is fresh. Return to room temperature before baking and increase the baking time to 25 minutes.

SAN MIGUEL'S CRABMEAT ENCHILADAS

1   cup sour cream
½   cup milk or half-and-half
    pinch of salt
1   pound sea scallops
3   tablespoons butter
1   tablespoon vegetable oil
1   pound lump crabmeat
1   clove garlic, minced

    vegetable oil
10 corn tortillas, preferably thin

Assembly and Presentation

1½–2   cups Monterey Jack cheese,
        grated

Variation

Mix together the sour cream and milk or half-and-half. Add a pinch of salt to taste. Set aside.

If the scallops are large, cut into small pieces. In a medium-size skillet, melt the butter and vegetable oil. Stir in the crabmeat, scallops, garlic, and half the cream mixture, reserving the remaining half for the topping. Cook about 3 to 5 minutes, stirring constantly over medium heat, just until the scallops are firm.

In another skillet, heat 1½ inches of oil to about 300°. Pass the tortillas into hot oil for a few seconds to soften and seal. Remove carefully and set aside between paper towels. Do this just prior to assembly.

Roll the crabmeat mixture into the tortillas and place side by side in a baking dish. Top with grated cheese, then the reserved sour cream mixture, and cover loosely with foil. Bake in a 350° oven for 20 minutes, then uncover and bake another 5 minutes.

I have soaked these enchiladas in 1 cup heavy cream for 2 hours before baking and found the results excellent. Try serving them on fresh, lightly steamed spinach leaves or fresh Texas watercress for a creative touch.

Fonda San Miguel

Storage, Freezing, and Advance Preparation

If using fresh crabmeat, the enchiladas may be filled, rolled, and frozen. Brush them with warm, heavy cream before freezing. Add the cheese and sour cream mixture after the enchiladas have thawed, prior to baking.

▼▼

Kokopelli, *Dallas*   Yield: 6 tacos

GRILLED SWORDFISH TACOS

Contemporary tacos are made with shellfish, duck, wild game, or seafood and are served with a variety of salsas. Chef Schindelheim's tacos are very light and make a good first course, or serve them on a bed of greens in place of a salad.

Cantaloupe Salsa

½	cantaloupe melon, diced ¼ inch
½	small, fresh pineapple, diced ¼ inch
½	red onion, diced ¼ inch
1	red bell pepper, diced ¼ inch
1	poblano chile, roasted, peeled, and diced
1	serrano chile, minced
2	tablespoons minced cilantro
	lime juice to taste
	salt to taste

Combine the salsa ingredients and gently toss. Season with lime juice, salt and pepper to taste.

2	4–5 ounce swordfish steaks
	olive oil
	salt and pepper

Preheat a grill to the highest heat. Brush the swordfish with olive oil and season with salt and pepper. Grill on both sides, about 8 minutes per inch of thickness. Remove and dice into ¼–½-inch pieces.

6	crisp taco shells

Fill each taco shell with warm swordfish and Cantaloupe Salsa. Serve on a bed on julienne spinach or mixed greens.

Via Real, *Dallas*   Yield: 4 servings

SQUASH ENCHILADAS

Via Real serves these light enchiladas with both a Sour Cream Sauce and a Chile con Queso Sauce.

Sour Cream Sauce

1	cup chicken broth
1	cup sour cream
1	tablespoon cornstarch
2	tablespoons water
½	teaspoon each, lime and lemon juice
	salt and pepper to taste

In a saucepan, bring the chicken broth to a boil. Dissolve the cornstarch in water, lower the heat and slowly add cornstarch mixture and sour cream to the chicken broth, stirring constantly, until thickened and smooth. Stir in lemon and lime juice and season to taste with salt and pepper.

Chile con Queso Sauce

1	tablespoon each, chopped green bell pepper, celery, onion, and jalapeño
1	Roma tomato, diced
½	cup water
¾	cup whipping cream
8	ounce Velveeta cheese, cubed
2	ounces grated cheddar cheese
2	tablespoons light olive oil
1	teaspoon minced garlic
1	cup chopped onion
4	cups sliced zucchini
4	cups sliced yellow squash
1½	cups diced Roma tomato
½	teaspoon each marjoram, thyme, and oregano
1	tablespoon chopped fresh cilantro
	salt and pepper to taste
8	corn tortillas
¼	cup grated cheddar cheese

To make the Chile con Queso, put the vegetables in a saucepan with the water and bring to a boil. Simmer until the water evaporates. Add the whipping cream and return to a boil, then add both cheeses and stir until melted. Keep warm until ready to serve.

Heat the olive oil in a large skillet over medium heat. Add the onion and garlic and sauté until onions are wilted. Stir in squash, tomato, and seasonings. Simmer over low heat about 10 minutes, or until vegetables are tender. Season to taste with salt and pepper.

Cover tortillas with plastic wrap and microwave about 2 minutes or until soft. One at a time, fill each tortilla with the squash mixture and place seam side down in an ovenproof casserole that has been lightly coated with a vegetable cooking spray. Coat with the Sour Cream Sauce, then the Chile con Queso. Top with grated cheese. Warm in a 325° oven 10–15 minutes, or until heated through.

CAFE NOCHE

Little Boats de la Noche (p. 169)

Main Dishes

HOT AND CRUNCHY TROUT
Hudson's on the Bend

ADOBE PIE
Blue Mesa

PAELLA LEVANTINA
Las Canarias

ACAPULCO K-BOBS
Ernesto's

POLLO PIBIL
Fonda San Miguel

VOODOO TUNA
Z-Tejas

GRILLED PEPPERS WITH CHICKEN
La Fogata

PECHUGA MONTEREY
Kokopelli

LITTLE BOATS DE LA NOCHE
Cafe Noche

CHILES EN NOGADA
Los Panchos

MARK'S CHILES RELLENOS
Mark Gonzales

CHICKEN ACAPULCO
Cafe Noche

SANTA FE CHICKEN
Cappy's

SHRIMP IN SALSA DIABLA
Mario's and Alberto's

GRILLED GOAT CHEESE RELLENO
Casa Rosa

LAS ESCALOPAS
Via Real

SHRIMP AND CORN CHILE RELLENO
Z-Tejas

SHRIMP AND CRABMEAT CREPES
Ernesto's

TORTILLA CRUSTED QUAIL
Hudson's on the Bend

TROUT TAMALE
Kokopelli

Pescado al Mojo de Ajo
Fonda San Miguel

Grilled Chicken and Corn Pasta
Blue Mesa

Marinero Fish
Mario's and Alberto's

Seared Achiote Halibut with Shitake
Z-Tejas

Mushroom Sauce
Z-Tejas

Stuffed Snapper
Ernesto's

Grilled Swordfish
Author's Contribution

Mario's Shrimp in Garlic Sauce
Mario's and Alberto's

Catfish with Tomatillo Sauce
Matt's Rancho Martinez

Chorizo Stuffed Pork Tenderloin
Z-Tejas

Marinade for Flank Steaks and Skirt Steaks
Author's Contribution

Marinade for Spit-Roasted or Grilled Chicken
Author's Contribution

Ninfa's Marinade
Ninfa's

Matt's Fajita Spice
Matt's Rancho Martinez

Matt's Finishing Sauce
Matt's Rancho Martinez

Beef Fajitas
Author's Contribution

Chicken Fajitas
Blue Mesa

Veggie Fajitas
La Hacienda

Red Snapper Fajitas
Casa Rosa

HOT AND CRUNCHY TROUT

Jeff Blank serves this in his restaurant with a Mango-Jalapeño Aoili under the fish and the Ancho Mayonnaise "streaked" on top. It is one of the most popular items in his cooking classes.

Ancho Mayonnaise

4	ancho chiles, stemmed, seeded
¼	cup pineapple juice
1	tablespoon brown sugar
1	cup mayonnaise
2	tablespoons powdered ginger
	salt and white pepper, to taste

2	cups corn flakes
¼	cup toasted almonds
¼	cup toasted sesame seeds
¼	cup sugar
1	tablespoon red chile flakes
1	tablespoon each salt and pepper

Cut or tear ancho chiles in small pieces and put in a small saucepan with enough water to cover. Bring to a boil and simmer until the chiles are very soft, about 10 minutes. Put soft chiles and 2–3 tablespoons of the liquid in a blender jar. Add pineapple juice and brown sugar and blend until pureed. Strain into a small bowl and add remaining ingredients. Set aside.

In a food processor fitted with the metal blade, pulse cornflakes, almonds, sesame seeds, sugar, and seasonings to a coarse crumb.

Egg Wash

4	eggs, beaten
1	cup milk
	flour, for the dredge
6–8	trout fillets, boneless, skinless
½	cup corn or peanut oil

Combine beaten egg and milk and put in a shallow bowl.

To bread the trout, dredge each fillet first in flour, then in the egg mixture, and finally in crumb mixture. Place a large skillet over medium heat and sauté trout fillets on both sides, until golden brown, about 2–3 minutes.

Serve the trout with a dollop of Ancho Mayonnaise and either Mango Salsa (p. 184) or Corn Relish (p. 185)

Yield: 8–10 large or 14–16 small

ADOBE PIE

This is the most requested recipe at Blue Mesa and one of the signature items in the restaurant. It does require a lot of preparation, but you can make both sauces 1–2 days in advance and the filling 1 day in advance. Use either small 8-ounce Pyrex molds or 12-ounce molds.

Ancho Chile Puree

8	ancho chiles
	water to cover

To make the chile puree, rinse the chiles and remove seeds and stems. Put them in a saucepan with enough water to cover and bring to a boil. Simmer, covered, for about 10 minutes. Let stand another 15 minutes. Put chiles in a blender and blend smooth. Use as much of the soaking water as necessary to make a smooth, moderately thick puree. Set aside 1 cup for the sauce and refrigerate the rest.

The Filling

3	cups chicken breast or thigh meat, grilled or roasted, diced
8	ounces shredded cheddar cheese
1½	cups cooked corn kernels (preferably grilled)
½	cup chopped cilantro, loosely packed
¼	teaspoon garlic powder
¼	teaspoon white pepper
2	poblano chiles, roasted, peeled, and diced

Combine the filling ingredients in a large bowl and set aside.

Blue Mesa

The Masa

3 cups masa harina
3 cups warm water
8 tablespoons vegetable shortening
16 tablespoons butter
1 egg
1 ounce chicken broth
½ cup chile puree (see above)
2 tablespoons salt
½ teaspoon cumin
2 teaspoons baking powder

Chile Cilantro Pesto (p. 26)

Enchilada Sauce (p. 34)

Chipotle Cream Sauce (p. 35)

To make the masa, combine masa harina and water, mixing well. In a food processor using the metal blade, whip the shortening and butter until light and fluffy. Add the masa and egg. Whip until fully incorporated.

In a separate bowl, combine the chicken broth, chile puree, salt, cumin, and baking powder. Slowly add to the masa mixture and whip until incorporated.

Spray 8-or 12-ounce bowls with a vegetable coating spray. Spread a thin layer of the masa in each bowl, spreading up the sides of the bowl, about ¼ inch thick. Spread about ½–1 tablespoon Chile Pesto on top, then the chicken filling almost to the top. Spread more masa on top to seal in the filling. Cover with a layer of foil.

Put the bowls in a large pan and fill it with hot water three-fourths of the way up the bowls. Bake at 350° for 45–55 minutes.

When ready to serve, unmold the pies and put on 8-or-10-inch plates. Fill a plastic squirt bottle with sour cream and set aside.

Ladle the Enchilada Sauce over each pie, then the Cream Sauce, to create a two-color effect.

Drizzle with sour cream.

▼▼▼

Las Canarias, San Antonio   Yield: 6 servings

PAELLA LEVANTINA

The very nature of paella makes the recipe somewhat inexact with regard to the liquid needed to finish the dish. Use your own judgment, adding enough to keep the rice from drying out, taking care not to overcook.

The Sifrito

1	pound pork tenderloin, cut in ¼-inch cubes
2–3	tablespoons olive oil
1	large onion, sliced
2	green peppers, thinly sliced
2	cloves garlic, minced
½	teaspoon salt
¼	teaspoon pepper
1	tomato, diced

In a large skillet, sauté pork in olive oil, adding onion and green peppers as the pork browns. Cook 3 minutes. Add seasonings and tomatoes. Remove from heat. This makes about 2½ cups.

The Paella

8	chicken pieces, preferably thighs or breasts
2–3	tablespoons vegetable oil
6	cups chicken stock
3–4	threads saffron
3	cups long-grain rice, cooked
3	lobster tails, meat removed
12	slices smoked Spanish sausage
12	clams, in shells
12	medium-size shrimp, peeled and deveined (leave tails intact)

In a large skillet, sauté the chicken in oil on both sides until brown, about 12 minutes. Set aside. The chicken will not be fully cooked.

Boil stock and saffron together for 2 minutes and let steep 5 to 10 minutes.

Place the sifrito, saffron, stock, rice, lobster, and sausage in a large baking dish or paella pan and bring to a boil. Arrange the chicken, clams, and shrimp on top of the other ingredients, and then bake, covered, in a preheated 375° oven for 20 minutes. You may need to adjust the amount of liquid as the paella bakes, adding more during the baking time or straining off excess if some remains after cooking.

▼▼▼

Las Canarias

Presentation

1   package frozen green peas,
      cooked
8–10 artichoke hearts, halved
      (optional)

Garnish the paella with cooked peas and/or artichoke hearts, if desired.

Author's Note

Cook the rice according to the package instructions, but reduce the cooking time by 8 minutes, so the rice is slightly undercooked. Sautéing the rice in a small amount of oil before adding the liquid will help prevent it from sticking together.

Storage, Freezing, and Advance Preparation

The paella may be frozen after the sifrito, rice, chicken, and sausage have been combined and partially cooked. Add the shellfish after thawing, during reheating. During the first baking, before freezing, reduce the time from 20 minutes to about 12. Paella is an excellent party dish and is easily prepared several days ahead, using several steps. This result will be better than freezing the paella. *The Day Before:* Prepare the sifrito. Cook the rice. Sauté the chicken, cooking slightly longer than the recipe suggests. *The Day of Your Party:* Assemble the dish for baking. Be sure the refrigerated ingredients return to room temperature before baking.

Ernesto's, *San Antonio*

Yield: 4 servings

ACAPULCO K-BOBS

Ernesto developed this unusual combination of beef, chicken, and shrimp, a typical Mexican-American grilled specialty. The unique butter sauce is his trademark.

The Sauce

2 green onions, thinly sliced
2 sticks unsalted butter, cut in 10 pieces
½ tablespoon vinegar
1–2 ounces orange liqueur
1 fresh pineapple slice, diced
½ tablespoon soy sauce
2 tablespoons shredded coconut, preferably fresh

In a large skillet over medium-low heat, simmer the green onions in 1 tablespoon butter, vinegar, and liqueur until soft. Add pineapple and then whisk in more butter, 1 piece at a time, over low heat. Do not allow the butter to simmer or it will separate. Whisk constantly to achieve a creamy consistency, lifting the pan from the heat if necessary to control the temperature. Stir in the soy sauce and coconut. The sauce may be held in a double boiler over hot water; however, do not place over heat.

2 seedless oranges
fresh lime juice
vegetable oil

Peel and halve oranges, cutting a thin slice from the base of each so they will remain flat. Grill the oranges on a roasting pan 4 inches from the broiling element. Brush with lime juice and oil and grill until hot and lightly browned. Keep warm.

The K-Bobs

½ pound beef tenderloin, cut in 1-inch cubes
2 boneless chicken breasts (singles), cut in 1-inch cubes
6 jumbo shrimp, peeled, deveined, and butterflied (leave tails intact)

For the k-bobs, use an outdoor grill with medium-hot heat or an indoor grill on highest heat. If necessary, k-bobs may be oven-broiled 4 inches from the broiling element; watch them closely so they do not burn.

▼▼▼

Ernesto's

The Basting Liquid

⅓ cup peanut oil
2 tablespoons soy sauce
   juice of 3–4 limes

In a small saucer, stir together the peanut oil and soy sauce for basting. Squeeze the lime juice into a separate saucer.

Assembly and Presentation

8 medium-size crisp white
   mushrooms
½ fresh pineapple, peeled and
   cut in 1-inch cubes

Alternate the beef, chicken, and shrimp with mushrooms and pineapple chunks on skewers. Brush liberally with lime juice and then with oil and soy sauce. Grill, turning to brown all sides, basting several times. Depending on the cooking source, time varies from 2 to 5 minutes per side. Transfer to serving plates and remove skewers.

2 cups cooked white rice
   prepared oranges
   minced fresh parsley

Serve the K-bobs atop the rice, lightly napped with sauce. Nap the oranges with sauce and then sprinkle with minced parsley.

Storage, Freezing, and Advance Preparation

The beef, chicken, and shrimp may be put on skewers earlier in the day. The sauce may be prepared 3 hours before serving and held over hot water (100° or less) or in a thermos bottle.

Fonda San Miguel, *Austin*   Yield: 6 servings

POLLO PIBIL

San Miguel serves an interpretation of Diana Kennedy's authentic recipes. Chef Miguel Ravago takes great pride in his food, and his own special touches make his dishes unique and delicious.

1	tablespoon achiote seeds
¼	cup water
¼	teaspoon cumin seeds
¼	teaspoon leaf oregano
3	whole allspice
4	cloves garlic, minced
1	tablespoon salt
¼	cup fresh orange juice
1	tablespoon red wine vinegar
6	chicken breasts (singles)
	banana leaves

2	tomatoes, peeled and chopped
1	1-pound can Italian-style tomatoes, including juice
1	large onion, thinly sliced
2	tablespoons vegetable oil

Presentation

fresh herbs
radish roses

At least one day ahead, cover the achiote seeds with ¼ cup water and bring to a boil. Soak overnight.

With a mortar and pestle or spice grinder, grind the seasonings together and then grind in the seeds with their liquid, orange juice, and vinegar.

Trim excess fat from the chicken and remove the skin. Spread with the achiote paste. Reserve about 1 tablespoon to finish the sauce. If available, wrap in banana leaves.

In a medium-size skillet, sauté the tomatoes with onion in hot oil until the onion is soft and translucent, about 8 minutes.

Stir in the reserved achiote paste and pour over the chicken. Cover with foil and bake 50 minutes to 1 hour at 350°.

To serve, transfer the chicken in the banana leaves to a platter. Return the sauce to a skillet and bring to a boil. Spoon over the chicken. Garnish with fresh herbs, such as parsley, cilantro, or watercress, and radish roses.

▼▼▼

Fonda San Miguel

Variation

This dish may also be served buffet style. Remove the chicken from the bone and cut into bite-size pieces, then combine with the reheated sauce. Serve with plain white rice and either green salad or fruit salad. Both pair nicely with the assertive seasonings of this dish.

Storage, Freezing, and Advance Preparation

The entire dish may be made ahead and reheated. It also freezes quite well; if serving buffet style, freeze before boning and cutting the meat.

▼▼▼

Z-Tejas, *Austin*   Yield: 4 servings

Voodoo Tuna

Both the sauce and the tuna have assertive pepper power, so this dish is not for the faint hearted. The Black Peppercorn Butter is delicious melted over char-grilled steaks, poultry, or fish.

Black Peppercorn Butter

2	shallots, minced
1	tablespoon coarse ground black pepper
¼	cup white wine
¾	pound unsalted butter, at room temperature
4	tablespoons chopped cilantro
4	tablespoons chopped basil
1	clove garlic, minced

To make the butter, bring the shallots, pepper, and white wine to a boil in a small saucepan. Boil until the liquid is nearly gone. Remove from heat, cool a few minutes and add butter, cilantro, basil, and garlic. Chill.

½	cup red wine
½	cup Balsamic or red wine vinegar
¼	cup sugar

In a small, saucepan heat the wine, vinegar, and sugar. Boil about 1 minute. Reduce heat and whisk in 4 tablespoons of the Black Peppercorn Butter and simmer 2–3 minutes.

4	7–8 ounce tuna fillets, about 1 inch thick
	Cajun "blackening" seasoning

Heat an ungreased cast-iron skillet over high heat. Lightly coat the tuna fillets with vegetable oil and dredge in blackening seasoning. Shake off the excess and sear the fillets about 5 minutes on each side.

Soy Mustard (p. 190)

Serve the fillets on top of the hot vinegar and wine sauce. Garnish with Soy Mustard.

La Fogata, *San Antonio*   Yield: 2 servings

GRILLED PEPPERS WITH CHICKEN

The attractive presentation of this off-the-menu dish is what has earned La Fogata its reputation for "nouvelle cuisine." This is a low-calorie recipe, particularly if served with a light tomato sauce. Be sure to note the oven method at the end of the recipe if you do not have an indoor or outdoor grill.

juice of 1 lime	Squeeze lime juice over the chicken breast. Season with salt and pepper. Grill over a moderate flame, brushing both sides with oil. When cooked and tender, about 12 to 15 minutes, remove the skin and shred the meat. Set aside. Or, bake in a 350° oven, seasoning in the same way, for 15 minutes.
1 chicken breast (single)	
garlic salt and pepper to taste	
oil	

2 large poblano chiles	Do not peel the peppers at this time. Wash them and then, using a sharp knife, make a circular cut to remove the stem in one piece, and set it aside. Remove the seeds and veins.

2 ounces Monterey Jack or mild Texas goat cheese, cut in small pieces	Stuff the prepared peppers with a combination of chicken and cheese, moistened with a scant amount of chicken stock. If using an open grill (indoor or outdoor), return the stuffed peppers to the grill and cook on both sides until the peel is charred. Take care not to burn. Remove, pulling away the peel, and then replace the top for garnish.
chicken stock	

Presentation

sour cream or salsa	Serve with sour cream or a light tomato salsa. Or note the creamy cheese sauce in the variation.

▼▼▼

La Fogata

Variation

I like to serve this dish with a sauce of sour cream and cheeses. In a small skillet over medium-low heat, stir together 3½ ounces cream cheese and 2 tablespoons grated Parmesan cheese until melted. Add ½ cup sour cream and continue cooking just long enough to heat through. Spoon over the peppers and, if desired, top with chopped pecans, lightly sautéed in butter.

Author's Note

If you do not have a grill, roast the poblano peppers (see p. 7) and then stuff with chicken and cheese. Brush lightly with melted butter and then bake in a hot, 400° oven for 12 to 15 minutes, or just long enough to heat the chicken and melt the cheese.

Storage, Freezing, and Advance Preparation

The chicken may be baked and the peppers stuffed a day in advance. They taste best hot from the grill, especially when cooked outdoors.

Kokopelli, *Dallas*   Yield: 4 servings

PECHUGA MONTEREY

Many restaurant recipes are difficult to duplicate at home because of the preparation of veal stock or other tedious restaurant preparations. This one makes a wonderful dish for entertaining, and while a little time-consuming, produces excellent results.

Tomato Salsa

1	large white onion, thinly sliced
2	cloves garlic, chipped
¼	cup olive oil
2	serrano chiles, roasted and peeled
1	small bunch cilantro stems
12	Roma tomatoes

Simmer the onions and garlic in 2–3 tablespoons olive oil until translucent. Add serrano chiles, cilantro stems, and tomatoes and simmer until tomatoes break open and are very soft. Puree in a blender until smooth. Remove and strain. Season to taste with salt and pepper.

Spinach

5–6	tablespoons olive oil
6	cups fresh chopped spinach
	salt and pepper
2	Roma tomatoes, diced
1	white onion, diced
2	cloves garlic, minced
½	teaspoon cumin
1	jalapeño chiles, stemmed, seeded, and diced
1	cup chicken stock
1	tablespoon cornstarch
	salt and pepper

Sauté the spinach in 1–2 tablespoons olive oil until wilted, about 3–4 minutes. Strain and reserve the liquid. Sauté the tomatoes, onion, and garlic in the remaining oil until the onion is soft and translucent. Add cumin, jalapeños, and reserved spinach liquid. Dissolve the cornstarch in chicken stock and stir into the mixture. Cook until thickened, about 2–3 minutes. Fold in the spinach and season with salt and pepper.

▼▼

Kokopelli

4 chicken breasts, boneless, skinless olive oil salt and pepper	Brush the chicken breasts with olive oil and season with salt and pepper. Grill on an outdoor grill, or sauté in equal amounts of butter and olive oil, in a large skillet, about 3–5 minutes per side.
4 ounces mild goat cheese	Put a large spoonful of the spinach mixture on top of each chicken breast. Top with goat cheese. Place under the broiler, about 8 inches from the element, to soften the cheese, about 1 minute.
Saffron Rice (p. 110) 1 cup sour cream 1–2 tablespoons milk	Serve the chicken atop Saffron Rice, in the center of the plate. Pool the rest of the plate with the warm Tomato Salsa. Dilute the sour cream with a little milk and drizzle over the entire dish.

▼▼▼

Cafe Noche, *Houston*   Yield: 4 servings, 3 "boats" each

Little Boats de la Noche

This signature dish from Cafe Noche may be served with rice, beans, and Pico de Gallo as an entrée, or as a "party food" on a buffet table. The Adobo Sauce gives the fish and beef its distinctive taste; however, you may substitute a hickory smoked barbecue sauce in its place, if desired.

16   dried corn husks, softened in
         hot water

Adobo Sauce

6–8   ancho chile pods
1–2   tablespoons vegetable oil
1½–2 cups chicken stock
         (more or less)
¼   cup orange juice
½   cup vinegar
2   cloves garlic, peeled
⅛   teaspoon oregano
⅛   teaspoon thyme
1   tablespoon salt
         honey to taste
         salt and pepper to taste

To make the sauce, place the chiles in a 300° oven for 5–8 minutes to "toast." Remove stem and seeds and cut in several pieces. Heat 1–2 tablespoons oil in a skillet and sauté the chile pods for a few seconds. Add about 1½ cups of the chicken stock and bring to a boil. Reduce the heat and add the orange juice, vinegar, garlic, and seasonings. Simmer over low heat until the chiles are soft, about 8–10 minutes. Transfer to a blender jar and blend until smooth, adding more chicken stock as needed. Strain. Adjust the sauce to taste with honey, salt, and pepper.

1   pound beef tenderloin, cut
       in ¼-by-2-inch strips
1   pound red snapper fillet, cut
       in ¼-by-2-inch strips
½   cup chopped cilantro
½   cup diced onion

Divide the sauce in half and marinate the fish and tenderloin separately for about 5–10 minutes. Combine the cilantro and onion and set aside.

▼▼▼

Cafe Noche

¼ teaspoon dried thyme
¼ teaspoon leaf oregano
½ teaspoon salt

Mango-Jicama Salsa

¾ cup diced jicama
¾ cup diced mango
2 tablespoons fresh lime juice
2 tablespoons fresh orange juice
2 tablespoons chopped cilantro
1 jalapeño, seeded and finely chopped
1 tablespoon vegetable oil
salt to taste

Remove the fish from the marinade and mix with half the cilantro and onion. Divide between 6 corn husks, roll to seal and tie both ends. (See note.)

Remove the beef from the marinade and sear in a hot skillet a few seconds. Combine with the remaining cilantro and onion and season with thyme, oregano and salt. Divide between 6 corn husks, roll to seal and tie both ends.

NOTE: Depending on the size of the corn husks, it may be necessary to use 2 husks to encase the filling.

Mix the jicama, mango, lime juice, orange juice, cilantro, and jalapeño in a glass bowl. Add oil and salt to taste.

Line the top of a steamer with a few softened husks and arrange the "boats" on top. Steam over simmering water, covered, about 8 minutes.

Heat the remaining sauce over medium heat to a boil. Remove the husks from the steamer and pull or cut open to make a "boat." Serve 3 per person, with additional Adobo Sauce and Mango-Jicama Salsa.

▼▼

Los Panchos, *San Antonio*   Yield: 6 servings

CHILES EN NOGADA

Araceli is locally famous for her version of this classic dish. I suggest toasting the pecans for a richer flavor and baking the chile instead of frying.

The Cream Sauce

½	cup heavy cream
1½	cups sour cream
	salt to taste
1	teaspoon fresh lime juice
1–2	tablespoons milk for thinning

Stir together the heavy cream, sour cream, salt, and lime juice. Let stand 2 to 3 hours at room temperature to thicken. Refrigerate but bring to room temperature when ready to serve. If the sauce is extremely thick, thin with milk.

The Picadillo

1	pound ground beef
1	clove garlic, minced
2	small onions, chopped
2	tomatoes, peeled and chopped
¼–⅓	cup dark seedless raisins
¼	teaspoon cinnamon
	salt and pepper to taste

In a medium-size skillet, sauté the beef with garlic and onions until lightly browned. Stir in the tomatoes, raisins, cinnamon, and salt and pepper to taste. Simmer about 10 to 15 minutes and then set aside to cool. Skim off excess fat.

The Chiles

6	poblano chiles, roasted and peeled

Roast and peel the chiles (see pp. 7–9). Using scissors, snip the seeds from the chiles, keeping the stems intact. Make an incision just long enough to allow filling. Stuff with the cooked and cooled beef mixture. If necessary, secure the opening with a toothpick.

Bake chiles in a preheated 350° oven until hot, about 15–20 minutes.

1	cup toasted pecans
½	cup pomegranate seeds, or sun-dried cranberries

Nap each chile with the cream sauce, and then garnish with both pecans and pomegranate seeds.

▼▼

Mark Gonzales, Chef, *Dallas*   Yield: 6 servings

MARK'S CHILES RELLENOS

Mark Gonzales, formerly from Popolos, a Mediterranean Bistro in Dallas, has a light and flavorful touch when preparing Mexican inspired dishes. Mark is from Los Angeles and has a passion for Mexican ingredients and a flair for their preparation.

1	cup cooked black beans, including about 2 cups of the broth or 1 16-ounce can black beans, including broth
1	clove garlic, minced
1	tablespoon orange zest
1	minced jalapeño chile, stemmed and seeded
	salt and pepper
2–3	tablespoons tamari sauce

If preparing the beans, soak them overnight in water to cover. Drain and put beans in a saucepan with enough fresh water to cover. Add double the amount of garlic, orange zest and jalapeño, plus ½ cup finely chopped onion and bring to a boil. Simmer for about 1 hour. Drain and set aside 1 cup beans and about 1½ cups of the broth. Note: If using canned beans, drain and reserve the broth. Add enough chicken broth to make about 2 cups. Bring the broth and bean liquid to a boil. Add garlic, orange zest, and jalapeño. Simmer for about 10 minutes, or until reduced to about 1½ cups. Season to taste with salt, pepper and tamari.

6	fresh poblano chiles
1	pound tuna or swordfish
	olive oil
	salt and pepper
½	cup cooked corn
¼	cup chopped scallions
1	clove garlic, minced
2	tablespoons extra virgin olive oil
2	tablespoons chopped cilantro

Remove seeds and stems from poblano chiles and cut a slit down the side to make room for the filling.

Brush the tuna or swordfish with olive oil and grill over a hot fire on both sides, for a total of about 8 minutes. Season with salt and pepper. Flake the fish with a fork. Combine the fish with corn, scallions, garlic, olive oil, and cilantro and mix well.

▼▼

Mark Gonzales

lime juice
salt and pepper to taste

Gently add the reserved black beans. Season to taste with salt, pepper, and fresh lime juice. Divide the stuffing between the poblano chiles and secure with 1–2 toothpicks to seal in the filling. Place chiles in the broth, cover and gently simmer or bake at 375°, until hot, about 12–15 minutes.

Serve 1 chile per person in shallow bowls with the broth.

Pico de Gallo (p. 24) or diced tomatoes

Garnish with cilantro sprigs, freshly chopped cilantro, and Pico de Gallo or diced tomatoes.

Cafe Noche, *Houston*   Yield: 6 servings

Chicken Acapulco

Cafe Noche is the result of owner Bill Sadler's own extensive traveling and tasting throughout Mexico and is highly praised by both local and national press. This popular entrée has all the elements that make Mexican food so appealing—color, chiles, and vivid flavor.

The Sauce

2	tablespoons unsalted butter
1	minced shallot
¼	cup white wine
¼	cup shrimp stock or clam juice (see note)
1½	cups whipping cream
¼	pound chopped shrimp
	salt and pepper to taste

To make the sauce, heat the butter in a small saucepan and sauté shallots over medium heat until translucent, about 1 minute. Add wine and shrimp stock or clam juice and bring to a boil. Boil until reduced by half the volume. Add cream and return to a boil, stirring occasionally. Boil to reduce again until thickened. Stir in the shrimp and reduce the heat to low. Season to taste with salt and pepper.

6	whole chicken breasts, about 8 ounces each
1	teaspoon garlic powder

Bone the chicken breasts, leaving the two halves attached and whole. Lay flat and pound between wax paper until evenly flattened, about ¼ inch thick. Take care not to break the skin. With the skin side down, sprinkle each breast with salt, pepper, and garlic powder.

6	poblano chiles, roasted and peeled
3	red bell peppers, roasted and peeled

Remove seeds and stems from chiles and peppers and lay flat. Leave poblanos whole, and cut red bell peppers in 4 equal strips. Lay a poblano on top of each breast, then put 2 red bell pepper strips on top.

▼▼

Cafe Noche

	safflower or vegetable oil
1	tablespoon minced garlic
1	cup diced onion
1	pound chopped fresh shrimp
¼	cup chopped fresh cilantro
	salt and pepper to taste
6–8	ounces grated Monterey Jack cheese

Heat 1–2 tablespoons oil in a small skillet over medium heat. Add garlic, onion, and shrimp and sauté a few minutes. Shrimp should not be fully cooked. Add cilantro and season with salt and pepper. Remove from the heat and mix in Monterey Jack cheese.

Divide the shrimp mixture between the chicken breasts. Roll up each one tightly and then tie in 3–4 places with string.

| 1–2 | tablespoons butter |
| 1–2 | tablespoons vegetable oil |

In a large skillet heat the butter and vegetable oil over medium high heat. Add the rolled chicken breasts and sauté to lightly brown all sides. Remove and place in a baking dish. Bake in a 400° oven for 5 minutes.

Assembly, Presentation and Garnish

Pool each serving plate with the sauce. Slice the chicken into ¼–½ inch slices and arrange on top of the sauce. Garnish with fresh cilantro sprigs.

NOTE: To make shrimp stock, clean shrimp shells and place in a sauce pan with enough water to cover. Simmer 10–15 minutes to make a light stock. Strain, pressing all juices from the shells.

CAFE NOCHE
Chicken Acapulco (pp. 174–175)

▼▼

Cappy's, *San Antonio*   Yield: 6 servings

Santa Fe Chicken

The combination of a richly flavored Black Bean Sauce, char-grilled chicken and Pico de Gallo is a winning combination of ingredients. Cappy adds a dollop of Avocado Butter and a well seasoned rice.

Avocado Butter

1	ripe avocado
½	tablespoon fresh lime juice
½	tablespoon fresh lemon juice
¼	pound butter
½	teaspoon lemon-pepper
	a few drops Tabasco sauce
	salt to taste

To make the butter, put the avocado in a food processor fitted with the metal blade. Add lime and lemon juice and blend. With the machine running, add the butter, in several batches, until incorporated. Add seasonings, mix well and adjust salt to taste.

6	whole chicken breasts
1	bottle Italian dressing
	salt and pepper

Marinate the chicken breasts in Italian dressing for 2–3 hours or up to 6 hours. Preheat an outdoor or indoor grill to the highest setting. Lightly season the chicken with salt and pepper and grill on both sides about 3 minutes per side. Remove and cut away center membrane.

Assembly, Presentation and Garnish

	Black Bean Sauce (p. 40)
1½	cups Pico de Gallo (p. 24)

Ladle the warm sauce on half the plate and place chicken on top. Serve a small dollop of Avocado Butter on top of the chicken with Pico de Gallo on the side.

▼▼▼

Mario's and Alberto's, *Dallas*   Yield: 3–4 servings, 1½–2 cups sauce

SHRIMP IN SALSA DIABLA

This is a spicy, garlic-flavored dish—a favorite of Mario Leal.

¼ yellow onion, chopped
2 cloves garlic, peeled and minced
1–2 tablespoons vegetable oil

Sauté the onion and garlic in hot oil until soft and translucent.

2 tomatoes, cores intact
3–4 chiles de árboles or small hot chiles such as japones, stemmed and seeded
3–4 cilantro sprigs
¼ teaspoon salt
¼ teaspoon white pepper

Meanwhile, place the tomatoes on a lightly oiled cookie sheet 4 inches from the broiling element. Leave the oven door ajar and turn the tomatoes to roast all sides. The skins will split. During the last few minutes, reduce the heat, add the chiles, and roast briefly about 2 minutes.

Transfer tomatoes, chiles, and all juices to a blender and puree along with cilantro, the garlic and onion mixture, and salt and pepper.

1 cup chicken stock
salt to taste

Return to a medium-size skillet and simmer with chicken stock for 15 to 20 minutes to thicken. Adjust salt to taste and then keep warm while preparing the shrimp. The sauce is somewhat thin; if you simmer it 15 to 20 minutes, it will thicken.

2–2½ pounds fresh medium-size shrimp
2–4 tablespoons garlic oil (see p. 193)
1 tablespoon fresh minced garlic fresh minced parsley

Peel, devein, and butterfly the shrimp, leaving the tails intact. In a large skillet, heat about ½ tablespoon garlic and half the oil and then sauté the shrimp for about 5 minutes. Turn over very briefly and then remove. Add more oil and sauté the remaining shrimp.

Serve the shrimp with the sauce accompanied by Mexican Rice.

Casa Rosa, *Dallas*   Yield: 6 servings

GRILLED GOAT CHEESE RELLENO

Casa Rosa grills the stuffed chiles for service; however, you may find it easier to heat them in the oven. This is a hearty dish, and will make a meal accompanied by a tossed salad and warm, soft tortillas.

6 poblano chiles, roasted and peeled vegetable oil	Lightly oil the chiles and quickly roast them over an open flame or on a rack over an electric burner on high. Take care not to overcook or the chiles become too soft to easily stuff. Rinse immediately under cold water and remove peel. Using scissors, make a slit down the center and snip away seeds and veins. Keep the stem intact.

10 ounces mild goat cheese, at room temperature
12 ounces shredded Monterey Jack cheese
⅓ cup Pico de Gallo (p. 24)

olive oil

Mash the goat cheese with a fork and combine with Pico de Gallo and Monterey Jack cheese.

Carefully stuff each chile with the cheese mixture and close with a toothpick. Brush the flesh lightly with olive oil and place in a baking dish. Bake at 400° for 10–12 minutes, or until the cheese is melted.

Assembly, Presentation and Garnish

5 cups Black Bean Chile (p. 93)
1½ cups corn kernels, grilled and cut from the cob
1 cup Pico de Gallo (p. 24)
sour cream, or Mexican Cream (p. 119)

Serve the Rellenos in a large, shallow bowl or plate and surround with warm Black Bean Chile. Garnish with grilled corn kernels and Pico de Gallo. Drizzle the Relleno with sour cream or the Mexican Cream.

▼▼▼

Via Real, Dallas   Yield: 6 servings

LAS ESCALOPAS

Skewers of scallops, tomatoes, and bell peppers are a popular, light entrée at Via Real. They may be grilled or broiled. The bacon adds flavor to the mild scallops and may be removed prior to serving.

Cilantro Cream Sauce

2	tablespoons unsalted butter
1	shallot, minced
⅓	cup dry sherry or vermouth
1	cup whipping cream
½	cup chopped cilantro
	salt and white pepper to taste

Heat the butter in a small saucepan over medium-low heat and sauté the shallot until translucent, about 2–3 minutes. Add sherry or vermouth and simmer 3–4 minutes. Stir in cream and cook over medium heat until thickened, about 5–8 minutes. Add cilantro and salt and pepper to taste.

6	skewers
30	medium-size scallops
10	strips bacon, cut in thirds
12	firm cherry tomatoes
2	green bell peppers, cut in 1-inch squares
1	onion, quartered and separated into 1-inch strips
	pepper

Rub the skewers with olive oil. Wrap a piece of bacon around each scallop and place scallops, tomatoes, bell peppers, and onion on the skewers. Brush the vegetables lightly with olive oil and season with pepper. Grill on a hot fire or under the broiling element of an oven. Turn often to grill all sides, about 8–10 minutes total time. Remove bacon and serve skewers atop rice.

	Saffron Rice (p. 110)
3	lemons, halves
	fresh minced, parsley

Drizzle the scallops with a small amount of sauce and garnish with fresh minced parsley and lemon halves.

Z-Tejas, *Austin*   Yield: 4 servings

SHRIMP AND CORN CHILE RELLENO

Contemporary chefs seem to prefer grilled or baked versions of Chile Relleno. This recipe combines shrimp and corn with the richly flavored poblano chile for a dish you can make at home.

4   poblano chiles, roasted and peeled

The Stuffing

1   tablespoon butter
¼   cup chopped green bell pepper
¼   cup chopped white onion
½   cup fresh corn kernels
½   pound cooked shrimp, peeled and chopped
1½ cups grated Monterey Jack cheese
    salt and pepper to taste

The Sauce

4   strips bacon, diced
1   small onion, diced
2   cloves garlic, minced
5   Roma tomatoes, peeled and chopped
1   cup chicken or beef broth
3–4 tablespoons chopped cilantro
    salt and pepper to taste
4   ounces grated Monterey Jack cheese

Carefully roast the chiles according to instructions on pages 7–9. Take care not to over "char" the chiles or the flesh will tear when peeled. Make a slit down the center of each one, using scissors. Snip away seeds and veins.

To make the stuffing, sauté the bell pepper and onion in hot butter over medium heat, until softened. Add the corn and cook 2–3 minutes. Remove from the heat and stir in the shrimp and cheese. Season to taste with salt and pepper. Divide the stuffing into 4 equal portions and shape into ovals. Stuff each chile, folding the flesh together to encase the stuffing. Secure with a toothpick.

To make the sauce, cook the bacon, onion and garlic in a medium skillet until browned. Add the tomatoes and broth and simmer until the sauce is thickened, about 15 minutes. Season to taste with salt, pepper, and cilantro.

When ready to serve, warm the chiles in a medium skillet in a small amount of hot butter or oil for 3–4 minutes. Transfer chiles to a baking dish, remove toothpicks and coat with sauce. Top with grated cheese and bake in a preheated 375° oven until the cheese is melted.

Serve chiles with additional sauce.

▼▼

Ernesto's, *San Antonio*   Yield: 12 servings

SHRIMP AND CRABMEAT CREPES VERACRUZANAS

This is a perfect example of Ernesto's masterful blending of classic ingredients in his own unique and innovative way. The results became one of his most popular new dishes.

The Crepes

1¾	cups flour
¾	cup milk
¾	cup water
4	eggs
1	teaspoon vanilla
½	stick butter, melted
	pinch of salt
	butter

Thoroughly mix or blend the flour, milk, water, eggs, vanilla, melted butter, and salt until smooth. Let the batter stand for 1 to 2 hours or refrigerate overnight.

To prepare the crepes, heat a dab of butter in a well-seasoned crepe pan. Pour about ¼ cup batter in the corner of the pan and then immediately tilt to cover the entire surface. When the top is no longer liquid, turn to lightly brown both sides. Be sure to place filling on the second side, leaving the attractive side visible.

Stack crepes and cover until ready to use.

The Sauce Veracruzana

4–5	scallions, sliced
1½	sticks butter, at room temperature
2	poblano chiles, roasted, peeled, and cut in ¼-by-1-inch strips

In a medium-size skillet, sauté the scallions in 1 tablespoon butter 5 minutes or until soft. Add the chile strips, cilantro, tomatoes, olives, and capers. Lower the heat. Whisk in the

▼▼

Ernesto's

4	cilantro sprigs, minced
2	tomatoes, peeled, seeded, and chopped
10	green olives, sliced
1	tablespoon capers

rest of the soft butter about 1½ tablespoons at a time, lifting the pan from the heat if necessary to prevent the butter from bubbling. Continue whisking until the sauce is smooth and creamy. Place over hot water, off direct heat, until ready to serve.

The Filling

12	medium-size shrimp, peeled and deveined
7	ounces crabmeat
12	crisp white mushrooms, sliced
2	tablespoons butter

Reserve 6 whole shrimp for garnish and then coarsely chop the rest. Sauté crabmeat, shrimp, and mushrooms in butter for 3 to 4 minutes. Stir in 3–4 tablespoons sauce Veracruzana. Set aside.

Assembly and Presentation

2	ounces white Mexican cheese or Monterey Jack cheese, grated
	reserved whole shrimp
	flour
½	tablespoon butter
½	tablespoon oil
	minced fresh parsley

Fill each crepe with 1–2 tablespoons of shrimp and crab mixture. Roll, folding the edges inward to encase the filling. Brush with sauce to prevent drying out. Top with grated cheese and bake in a preheated 350° oven until the cheese is melted, about 12 minutes. Meanwhile, dust the reserved shrimp lightly with flour and sauté in hot butter, oil, and parsley about 2 minutes. Nap the crepes with warm sauce and garnish every 2 crepes with 1 whole shrimp.

Storage, Freezing, and Advance Preparation

The crepes and filling may be prepared 12 hours in advance or prepared and frozen. The sauce will hold over hot water for 1 to 2 hours.

▼▼

Hudson's on the Bend, *Austin*   Yield: 5 servings

TORTILLA CRUSTED QUAIL

This same crust may be used for shrimp or fish. It is a popular restaurant method that is not too difficult to prepare at home.

Mango Salsa

2	ripe mangos, peeled and diced ¼ inch
3	Roma tomatoes, peeled, seeded and diced ¼ inch
¼	cup diced shallots
2	garlic cloves, minced
½	bunch cilantro leaves, minced
⅓	cup lime juice
2	tablespoons granulated sugar
1	jalapeño, seeded and diced (If you like the heat, leave in the seeds)
1	tablespoon white wine vinegar
	salt to taste

Combine the ingredients for the salsa and chill for 30 minutes.

Tortilla Crust

6	corn tortillas, fried crisp
1	tablespoon cayenne pepper
2	tablespoons chile powder
2	tablespoons lemon pepper
1/2	cup cornmeal
2	tablespoons garlic salt
10	quail breasts, boned
	flour, for dredging
	Egg Wash (p. 155)
	Baby lettuce mix
	Corn Pudding (p. 118)

Using a food processor fitted with the metal blade, process the ingredients for the tortilla crust to coarse crumbs.

Lightly dust the quail breasts in the flour, then in the egg wash, and finally coat both sides with tortilla crumb mixture.

Heat 1½–2 inches of peanut oil in a large skillet to about 325°. Pan fry the quail on both sides until the crust is set and lightly browned, about 4 minutes. Drain on paper towel.

Serve 2 breasts per person atop a mound of greens with Corn Pudding and Mango Salsa.

Kokopelli, *Dallas*   Yield: 6 servings

TROUT TAMALE

1   bunch dried corn husks

Poaching Liquid

7   cups chicken broth
1   cup white wine
1   garlic clove, chopped
1   bay leaf
1   teaspoon cracked black pepper
2   tablespoons each, diced carrot,
        onion, celery
1   jalapeño chile, minced
    juice from 1 lime

6   boneless trout fillets, about 8–9
        ounces each
6   tablespoons butter, at room
        temperature
    salt and pepper

Soak 14–16 large husks in hot water for about 1 hour or until softened. Discard silks and clean husks. Tear the small ends into about 1½-inch strips to "fringe." Lay the husks in a large rectangular casserole, overlapping with fringed ends on both sides. Combine all ingredients for the poaching liquid, bring to a boil, and pour it on top, filling about ⅓ of the pan. Lay trout fillets, skin side down, on the husks.

Dot evenly with butter and season with salt and pepper. Place in a 400° oven, cover with foil, and bake for 10 minutes. (Do not allow liquid to return to a boil.)

Corn Relish

1   tablespoon light olive oil
1   package frozen corn kernels
1   red bell pepper, diced ¼ inch
1   poblano chile, roasted, peeled,
        and diced ¼ inch
1   garlic clove, minced
1   tablespoon minced green onion
1   ounce tequila
1   teaspoon chile powder
    pinch oregano
    pinch thyme
    salt to taste

Heat the oil in a small saucepan. Add the relish ingredients and toss to heat and coat evenly with seasonings. Adjust salt to taste.

To serve the trout, arrange one corn husk on the plate with trout in the center. Spoon the relish partially over the trout. Drizzle with a little melted butter and fresh lime or lemon.

▼▼

Fonda San Miguel, *Austin*   Yield: 4 servings

PESCADO AL MOJO DE AJO

The sauce for this dish is like a French *beurre blanc*—opaque and creamy. Follow the instructions carefully to avoid overheating the butter and causing it to look clear or separate. Miguel leaves the garlic bits moderately coarse.

The Butter Sauce

1	clove garlic
1½	sticks butter, at room temperature

Heat the garlic with 1 tablespoon butter; do not allow the butter to bubble. Over very low heat, whisk in additional soft butter, about 1 tablespoon at a time, to make a smooth and creamy sauce. Lift the pan from the heat if necessary to avoid separating the sauce. Strain and then keep warm, off direct heat, so the sauce doesn't separate.

The Garlic Bits and Oil

1–2	tablespoons vegetable oil
4	large cloves garlic, coarsely chopped

In a small frying pan, heat the vegetable oil and sauté the garlic bits 5 to 8 minutes or until very lightly browned. Drain garlic bits on paper towels. Reserve garlic oil for another use.

The Fish

4	red snapper or swordfish fillets
	(approximately 8 ounces each)
	fresh lemon juice
	vegetable oil

Clean fish fillets and then squeeze lemon juice over each one. Brush both sides with vegetable oil. Broil fish with skin side down about 3 minutes. Turn and brush with garlic butter sauce; broil another 3 to 4 minutes until the fish flakes easily.

Fonda San Miguel

Presentation

reserved garlic bits
¼   cup fresh parsley, minced

Transfer fish fillets to a serving platter and garnish with garlic bits and minced parsley. A generous amount of fresh parsley complements (and tempers) the garlic.

Variation

I prefer to begin the butter sauce with ¼ cup each vinegar and white wine, which I simmer with 1 minced shallot for 3 to 4 minutes.

Storage, Freezing, and Advance Preparation

The butter sauce may be made 1 hour in advance and held over hot water or in a crockpot. However, for best results, prepare the fish just prior to serving.

▼▼

Blue Mesa, *Dallas*   Yield: 6–8 servings, 4 cups sauce

GRILLED CHICKEN AND CORN PASTA

The fresh corn flavors in the sauce for this pasta dish make it unusual and a delicious sauce for pasta and grilled chicken.

The Sauce

1½	cups fresh cooked corn kernels (divide use)
	chicken broth, if needed
2	cups Ranchera Sauce (p. 36)

To make the sauce, put 1 cup of the corn kernels in a blender and blend to puree. Add a small amount of water or chicken broth if necessary to aid blending. Add Ranchera Sauce and blend again until smooth.

1	cup heavy cream
½	cup tomato sauce
1	tablespoon leaf oregano
¾	teaspoon salt

Combine the corn puree with the remaining ½ cup corn kernels, cream, tomatoes, and oregano in a medium saucepan. Heat to a simmer and keep warm. Season to taste with salt.

2	pounds fettucine, preferably fresh

Cook the pasta al dente in boiling, salted water. Drain.

6	large boneless chicken breasts, about 3½ ounces each
	olive oil
	salt and pepper

Brush the chicken breasts with olive oil and season with salt and pepper. Grill or sauté over medium-high heat, on both sides, for 6–8 minutes or until fully cooked. Slice chicken diagonally into 4–5 pieces.

4	ounces Cotija cheese, crumbled
½	cup diced, roasted, peeled red bell peppers
½	cup whole, cooked black beans, unbroken
6	cilantro sprigs

Add the pasta to the heated sauce and toss to coat. Mound the pasta in 6 bowls and arrange the chicken around the edges. Garnish with cheese, roasted peppers, and black beans. Put a cilantro sprig in the center of each serving.

▼▼

Mario's and Alberto's, *Dallas*   Yield: 6 servings

MARINERO FISH

This specialty has been a favorite at both Mario's and Alberto's and Chiquita's for several years. It is worth the time involved in preparation. We found no loss of quality when substituting clam juice and water for fish stock, though watch the salt, as clam juice tends to be salty.

2 cups clam juice or fish stock 1 cup water	Bring the clam juice and water to a boil. Skim the foam that rises to the top and discard. Reserve the broth.
6 5–6 ounce fish fillets, preferably flounder or red snapper juice of 2 limes	Clean the fillets. Squeeze lime juice over them and set aside.
2 cloves garlic, minced 3 tablespoons fresh lemon juice ¼ teaspoon white pepper ½ stick butter 4 green olives, chopped 8 small shrimp, finely chopped ½ pound Velveeta cheese, cut in small pieces 1½ tablespoons cornstarch	In a 3-quart saucepan, combine fish stock (or clam juice mixture) with garlic, lemon juice, pepper, butter, olives, and shrimp. Bring to a boil and then reduce heat and simmer 10 to 15 minutes. Add the cheese in several batches, stirring until melted. Remove about ½ cup and dissolve the cornstarch in this liquid. Add and stir back into the sauce until thick and smooth. Set aside or refrigerate until ready to reheat and finish the dish.
1½ pounds fresh spinach, stemmed and chopped 1–2 teaspoons salt 1 clove garlic, minced 3–4 tablespoons safflower oil	Sauté the spinach in a large skillet with salt, garlic, and hot oil until tender and moisture has evaporated, about 3 to 4 minutes. Divide the spinach among the fillets and then roll up to enclose the filling. Secure with a toothpick if desired.
2 tablespoons butter, melted	Brush the fillets with melted butter. Bake in buttered warm ramekins 8 to 10 minutes at 350°. Reheat the cheese sauce over medium heat while the fillets are baking.
Presentation	Nap with warm cheese sauce just prior to serving.

Yield: 4 servings

SEARED ACHIOTE HALIBUT WITH SHITAKE MUSHROOM SAUCE

Achiote is a powder made from grinding annatto seeds. It was used traditionally to color rice or lard a bright yellow.

Soy Mustard

½	cup dry mustard
½	cup beer
½	cup Dijon mustard
¼	cup honey
3	ounces soy sauce

Combine the dry mustard with beer, Dijon mustard, honey, and soy sauce. Mix well and set 4 tablespoons aside for the sauce. Refrigerate the remaining Soy Mustard for another use.

4	tablespoons butter
½	pound shitake mushrooms, sliced
½	cup whipping cream

Sauté the mushrooms in hot butter until tender, about 2–3 minutes. Add cream and 4 tablespoons Soy Mustard. Simmer over medium heat 3–4 minutes or until thickened. Keep warm until ready to use.

4	7–8 ounce halibut fillets
3–4	tablespoons achiote powder
	salt and pepper

Score the halibut fillets crosswise with a sharp knife. Mix the achiote powder with enough water to make a thin paste. Spread thinly on both sides and season with salt and pepper.

Heat a small amount of oil in a large sauté pan. Sear the halibut on both sides over medium heat for about 3–3½ minutes per side.

Presentation

fresh minced parsley

Serve the fillets topped with the warm sauce. Garnish the plate with fresh minced parsley.

STUFFED SNAPPER

7 ounces lump crabmeat
2 tablespoons butter
2 snapper fillets (7 ounces each)
fresh lime juice
flour
salt and pepper
butter

Sauté the crabmeat in butter 2 to 3 minutes. Set aside.

Clean the fish and squeeze lime juice over each fillet. Halve the fish horizontally to make a cavity for the stuffing. Lightly flour the outside of each fillet, and then stuff with crab mixture. Close, sprinkle with salt and pepper, shaking off excess.

Bake in a buttered pan in a preheated 400° oven about 10 minutes. Brush with butter several times during baking. (Cooking time varies with thickness of the fish. When checking for doneness, remember the flesh should be just opaque but still appear quite wet.)

4 cloves garlic, finely chopped
1½ sticks unsalted butter, at room temperature
1–2 tablespoons fresh parsley, minced

In a medium-size skillet sauté the garlic in 1 tablespoon butter until soft, about 2 minutes. Whisk in the remaining soft butter, 1½ tablespoons at a time, over low heat. Do not allow the mixture to simmer, and continue whisking until smooth and creamy. Add minced parsley and set the sauce aside over a pan of hot water to keep warm.

Assembly and Presentation

minced fresh parsley
⅓ cup toasted almonds or pine nuts
2 cups cooked white rice

Nap each fillet with garlic butter sauce and then garnish with parsley and toasted nuts. Serve over rice.

▼▼

Author's Contribution Yield: 6 servings

GRILLED SWORDFISH

Swordfish is best grilled quickly over a hot fire or flat top. Serve with black beans or a black bean sauce and your favorite salsa.

6	fresh swordfish steaks, 1 inch thick (6–8 ounces each)
2	cloves garlic, minced
	fresh-ground black pepper

Rub the swordfish steaks with garlic and black pepper.

½	cup white wine
1	cup olive oil
2	tablespoons hot red chile pepper flakes
½	cup fresh lime juice
½	cup juice fresh pineapple juice
2	cloves garlic, minced
3	tablespoons soy sauce
¼	cup fresh minced cilantro
	Black Bean Sauce (p. 40)
	Cantaloupe Salsa (p. 150)

Whisk or blend all ingredients together. Place the swordfish in the marinade and rub both marinade and seasonings into the fish. Let marinate for ½–1 hour.

Prepare the grill, making a medium-hot fire. Grill 2 to 3 minutes per side. Season with salt and pepper. Remember the steaks will continue to cook after removal from the grill.

If using a griddle or skillet, sauté over medium-high heat in a small amount of clarified butter or half butter, half oil, for 2 to 3 minutes per side. Fish should be barely opaque, never dry, when done.

▼▼

Mario's and Alberto's, *Dallas*   Yield: 3–4 servings

MARIO'S SHRIMP IN GARLIC SAUCE

This is a recipe for garlic lovers. The crisp garlic bits are the secret . . . follow the instructions to the letter to avoid burning the garlic and spoiling the taste. The flavorful garlic oil that remains should be stored in the refrigerator and used for sautéing shrimp or any other meat or fowl.

12	cloves garlic, roughly chopped
1	cup vegetable oil
½	stick unsalted butter, cut in 4 pieces

In a large skillet, sauté the garlic in medium-hot oil (about 300°) until light brown. Watch carefully so as not to burn. After about 6 to 8 minutes, quickly whisk in the butter and remove immediately from the fire. When all the butter has been added, the bits will become crisp. Remove them with a slotted spoon and reserve the oil and butter for sautéing the shrimp. Note: this same oil is used with Shrimp in Salsa Diabla (see p. 178).

1½	pounds fresh medium-size shrimp, peeled, deveined, and butterflied (leave tails intact)
	salt to taste

In a large skillet, heat about 2–3 tablespoons of the reserved oil and then sauté the shrimp for about 5 minutes. Turn over very briefly and then remove. Add more oil as necessary to sauté all the shrimp. Salt to taste.

Presentation

minced fresh parsley
Mexican Rice (see p. 122)

Garnish with the garlic bits and parsley. Serve with Mexican Rice.

Variation

I like to brush the garlic oil over French bread, then sprinkle it with parsley and toast it. Serve this with the shrimp and accompany the dish with a lettuce-and-tomato salad.

Storage, Freezing, and Advance Preparation

The garlic bits may be prepared at least a day in advance, then toasted briefly under the broiler to crisp. The oil is then ready to use as desired.

Matt's Rancho Martinez, *Dallas*   Yield: 6 servings

CATFISH WITH TOMATILLO SAUCE

Most catfish is farm raised and has a sweet, light flavor and flaky white texture. It is delicious with the traditional Tomatillo Sauce on page 41.

6	6–8 ounce catfish fillets
	Fajita Spice Mix (p. 201)
	flour
2–3	ounces vegetable oil
	Matt's Finishing Sauce (p. 201)
6	tablespoons sour cream
	Tomatillo Sauce (p. 41)
6	ounces grated Monterey Jack cheese

Sprinkle catfish fillets with the Fajita Spice Mix on both sides. Lightly dust with flour, shaking off excess flour.

Heat the oil in a large cast-iron skillet over medium-high heat. Sauté the fillets on both sides until the flesh is flaky, about 5–6 minutes. Spoon 3–4 tablespoons of Matt's Finishing Sauce directly on the fillets and remove from heat. Transfer the fillets to a baking dish. Spread about 1 tablespoon sour cream on the top of each fillet. Top with warm Tomatillo Sauce and a generous tablespoon of grated cheese.

Advance Preparation

Place in a preheated 400° oven until the cheese melts, about 2–3 minutes. Serve immediately.

The Tomatillo Sauce and Matt's Finishing Sauce may be prepared a day ahead. The catfish can be sautéed 30 minutes prior to service and reheated. In this case, be sure the sauce is hot and increase the oven time to 8–10 minutes.

Z-Tejas, *Austin*

Yield: serves 4–6

Chorizo Stuffed Pork Tenderloin

The stuffing permeates the pork with flavor and seasoning. This is a good dish for entertaining. Serve it with fresh corn on the cob or your favorite cornbread recipe.

The Stuffing

4	ounces chorizo sausage, or spicy pork sausage
¼	cup chopped onion
1	poblano chile, roasted, peeled and chopped
4	ounces grated Monterey Jack cheese
2	whole pork tenderloins, about 1 pound each
	vegetable oil
	salt and pepper

To make the stuffing, remove the casing from the sausage and sauté over medium heat until fully cooked. Set aside about ⅓ for the sauce. Add the onion, poblano, and cheese to the remainder and mix well.

Trim both tenderloins, removing excess fat and silver skin. Butterfly each one by slicing down the middle, almost but not completely through the meat. Continue making small slices, taking care not to cut all the way through, until the meat is flat. Lay one tenderloin on a work surface. Spread the stuffing down the center. Put the other tenderloin on top and tuck in the sides to hold the stuffing in place. Tie together with string. Lightly coat with vegetable oil and season with salt and pepper.

The Sauce

6	cloves garlic, peeled
	(reserved) chorizo sausage
1½	cups whipping cream

Put the garlic in a small pan and coat with oil. Roast in a 400° oven until lightly browned, about 10 minutes. Cool and chop.

Z-Tejas

Heat a nonstick skillet over medium heat and sear the tenderloin for 2 minutes on each side. Roast in a 400° preheated oven for about 30–35 minutes.

Heat the cream in a saucepan to a boil. Boil for 6–7 minutes or until reduced and thickened. Stir in the garlic and reserved chorizo and cook, stirring often, until the sauce is thickened and smooth. Season with salt and pepper.

Slice the tenderloin in medallions and serve on top of the sauce.

▼▼

FAJITAS

The popularity of fajitas and their many variations has increased the demand for mesquite grilling, creating an interest in all-wood-grilled foods. I visited more than 50 restaurants in Texas and California that specialize in grilling, and the inconsistencies in both the grills used and the results were astounding. Everyone has a theory on marinades, dry seasoning rubs, wood versus mesquite charcoal (or a mixture of the two) and how to balance the different products over the same grill. There is no question, however, that food grilled over wood has delicious, aromatic flavors, and a wood fire produces a convected heat. That's why the food cooks faster and stays moist.

To most Texans, there's no mystery when it comes to grilling . . . it's almost inborn. "All it takes is a good hot fire and a steak." There is some truth in that statement. Skirt steaks—the traditional choice for fajitas—t-bones, or a rib eye are relatively easy to cook as they have enough fat to keep them from drying out, provided they are not overcooked. Marinades are used primarily for flavor or to tenderize tougher cuts of meat.

Grilling chicken, fish, or shellfish is another matter. There are three problems: absence of fat, overcooking, and the tendency for food to stick to the grill.

Several marinade recipes follow, all from different chefs. Here are some tips and techniques to keep in mind the next time you prepare fajitas.

1. When grilling skirt steaks, either tenderize or marinate the meat 4–5 hours or overnight before grilling.
2. Give a charcoal fire enough time to reach the proper temperature (hot!) and eliminate any "taste" if you used starter fluid.
3. Salt the meat, not the marinade.
4. Grill meat, chicken, and fish quickly, over a hot fire, basting with a marinade or basting sauce. This helps prevent the meat from drying out.
5. Always *undercook*, if you plan to use a sizzling presentation. Remember, meat, fish, and poultry continue to cook after being removed from the grill.
6. When pre-grilling the meat for a sizzling presentation, cover it to seal in the juices, and then cut in strips just prior to reheating.
7. Rub the grill with an oil-dampened cloth prior to building the fire. This prevents the meat from sticking. Using tongs, oil the surface again before putting meat or chicken on the grill.

Marinades, Seasoning Mixes and Sizzling Sauces

Marinades and sizzling sauces vary from Chef to Chef. Some are used for flavor, others to tenderize or add fat. Jesse Calvillo from La Fogata likes a marinade made with lemon or lime juice, Worcestershire Sauce, black pepper and peanut oil. Other chefs prefer to use lemon or lime after the meat or chicken has been cooked. Most agree a short (1–2 hour) marination is best when using high levels of citrus, or the meat will discolor, even toughen. Israel Jimenez from Blue Mesa likes a flavorful marinade made with beer, garlic, jalapeño chiles, onions and vegetable oil and Tony Fuentes from Casa Rosa uses a Chipotle Butter or soy and vinegar during grilling.

Marinano Martinez prefers to tenderize the meat with a dry spice mix and then dip the meat in the marinade prior to grilling. All methods produce excellent results.

Most restaurants simply drizzle clarified butter or margarine on the meat when it is put on the hot skillet for service. Some use a combination of melted margarine and soy sauce. Matt Martinez uses a combination of brandy, soy and vinegar. Some simply use fresh lime juice . . . healthier, but using a little hot fat produces the best sizzle.

Yield: About 5 cups or enough for
1 skirt steak (2½ pounds, more or less)

MARINADE FOR FLANK STEAKS AND SKIRT STEAKS

1	bottle Corona Beer
2	cups safflower oil
5	jalapeño chiles, stemmed and chopped
5	cloves garlic, minced
2	tablespoons black pepper
¼	cup soy sauce
3	tablespoons Worcestershire Sauce
3–4	cilantro sprigs, minced

Blend all the ingredients and place in a shallow glass dish, about 10 by 11 by 2 inches deep. Be sure to rub the marinade into the meat and turn it several times during the marinating time.

When using this marinade, be sure to generously salt and pepper the meat during grilling.

Yield: 5 cups

MARINADE FOR SPIT-ROASTED OR GRILLED CHICKEN

Marinate chicken 12–24 hours before grilling. If grilling boneless, skinless chicken breasts, baste several times during grilling. It is not necessary to baste spit-roasted chickens.

This marinade may also be used for beef or pork. Pork should marinate at least 24 hours.

3	jalapeño chiles, seeded and chopped
3	cloves garlic, minced
½	bunch cilantro, minced
2	cups safflower oil
¼	cup soy sauce
2	tablespoons Worcestershire Sauce
⅔	cup fresh lime juice
⅔	cup fresh orange juice
1	tablespoon fresh-ground black pepper

Blend the chopped jalapeños with the garlic, cilantro, oil, wine, and juices. Whisk thoroughly to blend ingredients. Rub the chickens with a little of the marinade and fresh-ground black pepper. Marinate at least 12 hours before grilling.

▼▼

Ninfa's, *Houston*   Yield: 1½ cups

NINFA'S MARINADE

Grilled meats and seafood are Ninfa Laurenzo's specialty—and one recipe has created her reputation. This marinade doubles as a glaze which may be used to brush the items during grilling.

1	stick butter or margarine
¼	teaspoon garlic powder
	juice of 1 lemon
	salt and pepper to taste
1	tablespoon cooking sherry
3	tablespoons teriyaki sauce

In a skillet or sauté pan, melt the butter. Stir in the garlic powder, lemon juice, salt and pepper, sherry, and teriyaki sauce. Simmer 2 to 3 minutes, stirring constantly to blend ingredients.

Matt's Rancho Martinez, *Dallas*

MATT'S FAJITA SPICE

4 tablespoons garlic powder
4 tablespoons kosher salt
4 teaspoons cornstarch
2 tablespoons paprika
2 tablespoons coarse-ground
    black pepper
¼ teaspoon white pepper
¾ teaspoon dried thyme

Combine all ingredients to evenly distribute spices and cornstarch. Use about 1 teaspoon per 3 ounces of meat. Rub the seasonings directly on the meat, then wrap the meat and refrigerate 4–5 hours or overnight.

Matt's Finishing Sauce

½ cup light soy sauce
2 tablespoons peach or cherry
    brandy
2 tablespoons red wine vinegar

Combine and drizzle on warm fajitas when they are put on the hot skillet. Use about 2 tablespoons per pound of meat.

Sizzling Sauce

⅓–½ cup soy sauce or
    Worcestershire sauce
½ cup chicken broth
½ cup white wine
8 tablespoons melted butter or
    margarine
    juice from ¼ fresh lime

Combine and use about 1½ tablespoons per pound of chicken, beef or fish. Use as above.

▼▼▼

Author's Contribution   Yield: 4 servings

BEEF FAJITAS

This is a method rather than a "recipe," combining the various techniques and suggestions from different chefs. Fajitas are simply grilled skirt steaks cut in strips and served on a hot skillet with peppers and onions.

The Accompaniments

Guacamole (p. 32)
sour cream
Pico de Gallo (p. 24)
grated cheese
lettuce, thinly sliced
Refried pinto or black beans

Prepare the Guacamole and Pico de Gallo and refrigerate until ready to serve. Arrange lettuce and sour cream on individual serving plates.

The Meat

skirt steak or
beef tenderloin

If using skirt steak, trim some of the fat and sprinkle on both sides with a seasoning mix, Fajita Spice (p. 201), or tenderizer. Cover and refrigerate 6–8 hours. (It is not necessary to use tenderizer with beef tenderloin.)

Prepare a liquid marinade using garlic, Worcestershire or soy sauce, minced serrano chiles, and a light oil, or choose from the marinades on pp. 199–200, 204. Dip the meat in the marinade and grill over a hot fire on both sides to medium rare. Season with salt and pepper during grilling. Cut the meat into strips.

Author's Contribution

The Onions and Peppers

red or white onions, cut in strips
green, red, and yellow bell
   peppers, cut in strips

Sizzling Sauce (p. 201)
flour or corn tortillas
fresh lime wedges

Sauté the onions and peppers in a hot skillet over medium-high heat until lightly browned. For service, heat a fajita skillet over medium-high heat. Add a small amount of oil and quickly stir-fry the meat strips to reheat. Push the meat strips to one side and add the onions and peppers. Drizzle with a small amount of melted margarine or a sizzling sauce and serve with warm tortillas, lime wedges, and refried beans. Put a scoop of Guacamole and Pico de Gallo on the small plates with lettuce and sour cream.

CHICKEN FAJITAS

Most restaurants serve fajitas with the same accompaniments but vary in their marinades and sizzling sauces or techniques. This is how Chicken Fajitas are prepared at Blue Mesa. The achiote marinade is what gives them their distinctive color.

Achiote Basting Marinade

3	ounces achiote paste
3	ounces orange juice
2	cloves finely minced garlic
1	teaspoon leaf oregano

Combine the ingredients for the achiote marinade and set aside. You will use this to baste the chicken during grilling.

Fajita Marinade

1	can Tecate Beer
1½	cups corn or vegetable oil
¼	cup fresh lime juice
3	cloves minced garlic
1	cup diced onion
3	jalapeño chiles, halved
	several sprigs fresh cilantro
8	chicken breasts, skinless, boneless
	kosher salt
	coarse ground pepper
1	onion, sliced
1	each red, green, and yellow bell peppers, sliced

Combine the marinade ingredients in a shallow glass dish. Marinate the chicken for 2–4 hours, but not more than 6 hours. Preheat a grill to the highest setting and grill the chicken on both sides. Season with kosher salt and pepper and brush with the achiote marinade during grilling. Grill until slightly undercooked, about 6–8 minutes. Cover and keep warm while preparing the peppers.

Heat a small amount of oil in a large skillet and sauté the peppers and onions until lightly browned. Put the peppers on a heated fajita or iron skillet. Cut the chicken into strips and reheat in a clean, hot skillet. Mound on top of the peppers and onions.

▼▼

Blue Mesa

melted margarine
fresh lime half

Guacamole (p. 32)
Pico de Gallo (p. 24)
sour cream
iceberg lettuce, thinly sliced

12 flour tortillas

To serve, heat the margarine to a sizzle and drizzle over the chicken and onions. Serve with fresh lime half and accompaniments: Guacamole, Pico de Gallo, sour cream, lettuce, and warm tortillas.

Mariano's La Hacienda, *Dallas*   Yield: 4 servings

VEGGIE FAJITAS

Mariano was one of the first restaurateurs to put sizzling fajitas on his menu at Mariano's in Dallas. This restaurant later became "On the Border" and is famous for fajitas. His fajita spice mix is a well-guarded secret; however, you can try the one on page 201 or choose from the many spice mixes now available in super-markets. The vegetables can be grilled or sautéed . . . this is a festive way to eat healthy! Almost all restaurants have some vegetable dish. This is fun because you can use whatever vegetables you like and roll them in tortillas with a variety of sauces or salsas.

1	tablespoon vegetable oil
2	tablespoons margarine
3	cups broccoli florets, blanched
3	cups cauliflower florets, blanched
2	yellow squash, cut on the diagonal
3	zucchini squash, cut on the diagonal
2	red bell peppers in thick slices
1	red onion thickly sliced

salt and pepper

Salsa de Tomatillo (p. 42)
sour cream
grated Monterey Jack cheese
Mexican Rice (p. 122)
warm flour tortillas

Garnish

tomato wedges
Pico de Gallo (p. 24)

Heat the margarine and oil in a large skillet over medium heat. Add the vegetables and stir-fry over medium heat until lightly browned but still crisp. Season with salt and pepper.

Heat a fajita skillet over medium-high heat. Place the sautéed vegetables on the hot skillet, toss and drizzle with a few teaspoons of melted margarine. Serve with Tomatillo Sauce, sour cream, grated cheese, Mexican Rice, and flour tortillas.

NOTE: Mariano serves the vegetables on a bed of Mexican Rice at La Hacienda. It's not necessary to "sizzle" these on a fajita skillet, but it does enhance the presentation.

Casa Rosa, *Dallas*

Yield: 4 servings

RED SNAPPER FAJITAS

Any firm-flesh fish such as swordfish or tuna may be used.

Chipotle Butter

1	pound melted butter or margarine
½	can chipotle chiles
¼	cup fresh lemon juice
1	tablespoon fresh minced dill
1	teaspoon tarragon
2	teaspoons white pepper
	pinch of salt
¼	cup milk

To make the chipotle butter, blend the ingredients in a blender to combine. Warm the butter in a small saucepan and use to baste the fish.

4	8-ounce red snapper fillets
	salt and pepper

Season the snapper fillets with salt and pepper. Preheat an outdoor or indoor grill to high. Rub the grill rack with an oil-dampened cloth to keep the fish from sticking. Grill the snapper on both sides, about 3–4 minutes per side. Baste often with melted chipotle butter.

1	red onion, sliced in strips
1	white onion, sliced in strips
1	red bell pepper, cut in strips
1	green bell pepper, cut in strips
1	yellow bell pepper, cut in strips
	vegetable oil

Heat a large iron skillet over medium-high heat. Add 1–2 tablespoons vegetable oil and sear the peppers and onions until lightly browned and softened, about 4–5 minutes. Cut the fillets in thirds and serve on top of onions and peppers. Drizzle with a small amount of chipotle butter.

Bottom: Chocolate Mousse Taco (pp. 225–226), Blue Mesa; *Left:* Cajeta Crepes (p. 210),
Ernesto's; *Top left:* Capirotada (p. 214), Author's Contribution; *Right:* Chocolate Bread Pudding
(p. 228), Kokopelli

DESSERTS

CAJETA CREPES
Ernesto's

SOPAIPILLAS
La Hacienda

APPLE ZAPATA WITH TEQUILA
SABAYON
Cafe Noche

CAPIROTADA
Author's Contribution

BANANAS MARGARITA
Cappy's

MARIANO'S FRUITCAKE
Mariano's

LIME CUSTARD WITH CREME FRAISE
Hudson's on the Bend

FRESH BERRY NACHOS
Author's Contribution

ALMOND FLAN
Fonda San Miguel

HONEY FLAN
Blue Mesa

PRALINE DESSERT
La Esquina

COFFEE TOFFEE PIE
Fonda San Miguel

CHOCOLATE MOUSSE TACOS
Blue Mesa

PINEAPPLE AND ORANGES TEQUILA
Author's Contribution

CHOCOLATE BREAD PUDDING
Kokopelli

TOASTED COCONUT CUSTARD
WITH CAJETA
Boudro's

TEXAS SOPAIPILLAS
Matt's Ranchero

MEXICAN NUT COOKIES
Author's Contribution

▼▼

Ernesto's, *San Antonio*   Yield: 8 servings

CAJETA CREPES

The cajeta sauce is made fresh by Ernesto for his crepes (see p. 182). You may use a prepared sauce; however, your result will be more like a caramel sauce. Simply mix with cream and brandy to a pourable consistency.

2 quarts whole milk 3 cups sugar ¾ teaspoon baking soda	In a large stockpot, stir together the milk, sugar, and baking soda to dissolve the sugar. Then bring to a boil over medium-high heat. Simmer, stirring occasionally, for 4 to 5 hours or until very thick and caramel in color. Refrigerate until ready to use.
1½ cups pecans, chopped 2 tablespoons butter	Sauté the pecans in butter and then place in a 350° oven and toast until crisp, about 8 minutes. Set aside.

Assembly and Presentation

2 ounces brandy 8 crepes (see p. 182)	When ready to serve, reheat about 1½ cups of the sauce in a 12-to-14-inch skillet along with the pecans and brandy. When the sauce simmers, add 1 crepe at a time, using tongs or 2 forks to fold into a triangular shape. When all are folded, remove from heat and transfer to serving dishes. Spoon additional sauce over each serving, and garnish with pecans.

Storage, Freezing, and Advance Preparation

The sauce may be made 2 days ahead and refrigerated until ready to use.

▼▼▼

La Hacienda, *San Antonio*   Yield: 6 Sopaipillas

SOPAIPILLAS

These delicious puffs of pastry may be served with meals or dipped into confectioner's sugar and served for dessert with honey or fruit butters. Be sure to note the technique of spooning hot oil over the sopaipillas as they fry. This ensures that they will puff and be light.

1	cup all-purpose bleached flour
2	teaspoons baking powder
1	teaspoon salt
1	tablespoon sugar
1	tablespoon vegetable shortening
⅓	cup hot water
1–2	tablespoons flour, if needed

Put the flour, baking powder, salt, sugar, and shortening in a mixing bowl. Use your fingers or a pastry blender to thoroughly combine and evenly distribute shortening.

Add hot water and stir with a fork until mixture forms a dough. If dough is too dry to mold or knead, add a bit more water. If dough seems too wet, add 1–2 tablespoons flour. Knead a couple of times, then place in a plastic bag and let rise 1 hour in a warm place.

Lightly flour a work surface and roll dough into a rectangle about ⅛ to ¼ inch thick. If the dough seems too elastic to roll easily, cover and let rest a few minutes more, then roll again. Fold the dough in half and roll the rectangle again. Cut the dough into 3-by-4-inch rectangles.

peanut oil for frying
powdered sugar
honey

Heat at least 5 inches of oil in a 3-quart saucepan or deep-fryer to 350° to 360°. Fry 1 or 2 at a time, spooning hot oil over the top to encourage puffing. Drain on paper towels. Immediately dust with powdered sugar and serve with honey.

▼▼

La Hacienda

Author's Note

I like to serve these with homemade fruit butters. The orange mango butter is one of my favorites.

Orange Mango Butter

	zest from 1 orange
8	ounces cream cheese
1½	sticks unsalted butter
6–8	tablespoons powdered sugar
1	fresh mango or papaya, diced

Thoroughly cream the zest, cream cheese, butter, and powdered sugar. Blend in diced fruit. You may substitute canned mango, well drained, for the fresh.

Honey Pineapple Butter

	zest from 1 orange
½	cup fresh pineapple, pureed
1½	cups creamy honey
1½	sticks unsalted butter
½	teaspoon vanilla
4–6	tablespoons powdered sugar

Thoroughly cream all the ingredients to make a smooth butter. Adjust the amount of sugar to personal taste.

Storage, Freezing, and Advance Preparation

Sopaipillas may be made several hours ahead but should be fried just prior to serving. The butters may be made a day in advance.

▼▼▼

Cafe Noche, *Houston*   Yield: 6–8 servings

APPLE ZAPATA WITH TEQUILA SABAYON

The sauce for this dessert is good enough to eat by itself. You can serve it with berries, a chocolate cake, or fresh fruits. You may substitute frozen pastry, thawed and cut in rounds, for the fresh flour tortillas.

Tequila Sabayon

4 egg yolks, at room temperature 1 cup sugar ⅛ cup tequila	In the top of a double boiler, over simmering water, beat the egg yolks, sugar, and tequila until very thick and creamy, about 6–8 minutes. Remove from heat and let cool 15–20 minutes.
2 cups whipping cream	Whip the cream until stiff. Whip the egg yolk mixture once again and then fold the two mixtures together. Refrigerate.
4 cups chopped, peeled apples ¼ teaspoon cinnamon ½ cup sugar ½ cup cornstarch 1 cup water ½ cup seedless raisins ½ cup toasted, chopped walnuts	Mix the apples, cinnamon, and sugar in a saucepan. Cook over medium-low heat until apples are soft. Combine cornstarch and water and stir into the apple mixture. Cook until thick and clear. Add raisins and walnuts. Remove from heat and cool.
4 ounces cream cheese, cut in cubes	
6–8 fresh, uncooked, flour tortillas or pastry cut into 5–6-inch circles	Spoon the filling on top of each tortilla or pastry round. Top with a few cubes of cream cheese. Fold over and crimp the edges to seal. Brush with melted butter and cinnamon sugar. Bake in a preheated 450° oven for 10–15 minutes, or until lightly browned. Serve warm with chilled Tequila Sabayon.

▼▼

Author's Contribution   Yield: 8 servings

CAPIROTADA

Many bread puddings are made with a sugar syrup in place of cream. This is my adaptation of an authentic recipe that has a cream and sugar syrup.

⅔   cup almonds or pecans, coarsely chopped
1½ cups apples, chopped
½   cup golden seedless raisins

Combine nuts, apples, and raisins. Set aside.

1   cup brown sugar, firmly packed
¾   cup water
2   tablespoons sherry (optional)
2   sticks cinnamon
1   whole clove
1   teaspoon anise seeds
½   cup whipping cream

In a medium-size saucepan, combine sugar, water, sherry, if desired, cinnamon sticks, clove, and anise seeds and bring to a boil over medium-high heat. Let boil 2 minutes. Strain and set aside. When cool, mix in cream.

5   day-old sweet Mexican breads or soft rolls, about 5 cups bread cubes
1   stick butter

Preheat oven to 350°. Butter a 1½-quart casserole (at least 3 inches deep) or soufflé dish. Trim thin portion of top and bottom crusts from the Mexican pastry, if using. Cut it into ½-inch-thick slices. Melt about 5 tablespoons butter in a large skillet over medium-high heat. Add pan dulce or bread slices in batches and sauté on both sides until golden, about 2 minutes, adding more butter if necessary. Remove from skillet. Melt the remaining butter.

4   ounces queso fresco or cream cheese, chilled and crumbled

Arrange ⅓ of the bread in the prepared dish. Cover with ½ of the nut filling. Sprinkle with ½ of the cheese, then drizzle with ½ of the syrup. Repeat layering twice, alternating slices to cover empty spaces. Pour remaining melted butter over top. Press down gently on slices to soak well.

Bake at 350° for 30–35 minutes. Serve warm with whipped cream.

▼▼

Cappy's, *San Antonio*   Yield: 6 servings

BANANAS MARGARITA

Cappy Lawton, an inventive and passionate cook, created this delicious dessert which will remind you of the New Orleans specialty, Bananas Foster, with a Tequila "kick." The sauce may be made in advance, but the dessert needs to be finished and assembled prior to service.

The Sauce

1	cup tequila
¼	cup triple sec liqueur
2	cups brown sugar, packed
¾	cup fresh lime juice
	zest from 4–5 limes
6	tablespoons butter

To make the sauce, pour the tequila and triple sec in a saucepan over high heat (being careful not to burn yourself or anyone else) to burn off the alcohol. High heat will cause a flame, but you can just simmer the mixture for 6–8 minutes or until the liquid is reduced to about ½–⅓ cup. Stir in the brown sugar and cook until dissolved and light amber in color, about 5 minutes. Add the lime juice and zest and simmer until reduced, about 18 minutes. Stir in the butter and remove from heat once the butter is incorporated.

7–8	bananas, ripe but firm
6	scoops vanilla ice cream

When ready to serve, reheat the sauce. Halve the bananas and warm the halves in the sauce for 4–5 minutes. Place bananas on a serving plate with a scoop of ice cream. Pour the sauce over the ice cream and bananas.

Presentation

¾	cups toasted chopped pecans
6	mint sprigs

Garnish each plate with toasted pecans and a mint sprig.

▼▼

Mariano's, *Dallas*   Yield: 1 large cake, 2 mini-loaves

MARIANO'S FRUITCAKE

This is a prized recipe from Mariano's father, who is responsible for many of the delicious recipes in Mariano's restaurants. I have taken the liberty of substituting Mexican candied fruit for the standard candied fruit mix which somehow seems natural. The cake keeps moist for several months, particularly when soaked with the optional glaze. Mini-loaves of this cake make an excellent gift.

½	pound dark seedless raisins
1	pound candied pumpkin or candied papayas, cut in small pieces
1	pound dates, snipped
½	pound candied cherries
¼	pound candied citron, cut in small pieces
½	pound candied pineapple or candied oranges, diced
¼	pound candied sweet potatoes, cut in small pieces
1	pound pecans, walnuts, pine nuts, almonds, or any combination of nuts, chopped
¼	cup bourbon

At least 2 hours ahead or overnight, soak the fruits and nuts in bourbon, stirring several times. Reserve several whole nuts for the garnish.

2	sticks unsalted butter
½	pound brown sugar (about 1 cup plus 3 tablespoons), loosely packed
8	eggs, separated

Butter an angel food cake or bundt pan and set aside.

In a large bowl, cream the butter with the brown sugar. Add the egg yolks, 2 at a time, beating after each addition.

▼▼

Mariano's

2	cups unbleached all-purpose flour
½	tablespoon cinnamon
½	tablespoon ground cloves
½	tablespoon allspice
½	tablespoon ground coriander or mace
½	tablespoon nutmeg
½	teaspoon salt
¼	cup red wine
¼	cup orange juice concentrate

Sift together the flour and spices. Add to the egg mixture along with the wine and orange juice concentrate.

In a separate bowl, beat the egg whites until stiff but not dry; then fold into the batter alternately with the fruits and nuts.

Transfer the batter to the prepared pan and bake in a preheated 250° oven for 3 hours. The extra batter may be baked in miniloaf pans along with the cake. Take them out 30 to 35 minutes before the large cake. Garnish with whole nuts.

Optional Glaze

2	medium-size oranges
½	cup granulated sugar
6	tablespoons butter
⅓	cup bourbon

Using a stripper, remove peel from both oranges and set aside. Squeeze all the juice into a medium-size skillet along with the sugar, butter, and bourbon and bring to a boil. Add the strips of peel and simmer about 4 to 5 minutes. Cool 5 minutes; then spoon over warm cake, using a rack for the cake. Reserve the juice; then spoon over the cake again, repeating the procedure until all the glaze is absorbed. Wrap the cake in a damp towel and remoisten every few days.

Storage, Freezing, and Advance Preparation

The fruits and nuts may be prepared a day ahead. I usually do this in addition to measuring all the ingredients. The cake is best made several weeks prior to serving. I like to glaze the cake, then wrap it for seasoning for about 4 weeks. It is delicious served within 1 or 2 days but slices better after 3 days.

Hudson's on the Bend, *Austin*   Yield: 6–8

LIME CUSTARD WITH CREME FRAISE

While the origins of this recipe are from an American State Fair (and not Mexican), it makes a wonderfully light and refreshing finale to a spicy Mexican meal. The "custard" forms a light cake with a lemon custard on the bottom.

Creme Fraise

1   cup heavy cream
3   tablespoons buttermilk
    sugar to taste
    a few drops vanilla extract

To make the Creme Fraise, combine the cream and buttermilk and refrigerate overnight. Mix in sugar to taste and vanilla extract.

The Custard

¾   cup sugar
1½ tablespoons butter
2   teaspoons grated lime zest
3   eggs, separated
3   tablespoons flour
¼   cup fresh lime juice
        (Mexican limes)
1   cup whole milk

To make the custard, cream together ½ cup sugar, butter, and lime zest. Add egg yolks and beat well. Add flour a little at a time, alternating with lime juice and milk.

In a separate bowl, beat the egg whites until stiff but not dry. Gradually add the remaining ¼ cup sugar. Fold the egg whites into the batter. Pour the batter into a buttered 9-inch round cake pan.

Place the pan in a larger pan filled with 1 inch hot water. Bake at 350° for 50–60 minutes of until set. Cool several minutes before cutting into wedges. Sift powdered sugar on top.

Fresh assorted berries
    (raspberries, blueberries,
    blackberries)
powdered sugar

Serve the dessert warm or cold with Creme Fraise and fresh berries.

NOTE: This may also be baked in custard cups. In this case, do not unmold but serve Creme Fraise and berries on the side.

Yield: 4 servings

Fresh Berry Nachos

Variations on this theme pop up on several different restaurant menus. This is a fun, colorful dessert that is easy to prepare and fun to share. When berries are not in season, use any colorful fruit combination.

2	cups sugar
1	tablespoon cinnamon

Combine the sugar and cinnamon in a large bowl.

12–16	flour tortillas each one cut in six wedges
3	cups peanut oil for frying

Heat the peanut oil in a medium saucepan over medium-high heat to 350°.

Deep fry the tortilla wedges in several batches, until crisp and lightly browned. Remove with tongs and immediately coat with cinnamon sugar. Cool and place in a sealed container.

	Cajeta Sauce (pp. 210 or 229)
	Creme Fraise (p. 218) or sweetened whipped cream
1	pint fresh raspberries
2	pints fresh blueberries
12	strawberries, quartered chocolate fudge sauce

Prepare the Cajeta Sauce and keep warm. Heat the chocolate fudge sauce and keep warm or at room temperature. Prepare the Creme Fraise or whipped cream and place in a plastic squirt bottle.

To assemble the dessert, divide the cinnamon-coated tortillas between four dinner-size plates. Scatter assorted berries generously on top. Drizzle the berries with chocolate sauce and Cajeta Sauce. Using the squirt bottle, make a decorative garnish with the Creme Fraise.

Serve the tart with a dollop of Ancho Mayonnaise and either Mango Salsa (p. 184) or Corn Relish (p. 185).

Fonda San Miguel, *Austin*

Yield: 8 servings

ALMOND FLAN

The nuts form a crust when the flan is unmolded. If you prefer to omit the nuts, you need not change any other ingredients.

2	tablespoons water
½	cup granulated sugar

Stir water into sugar and then, using an 8-to-9-inch skillet, bring the mixture to a boil. Use a brush dipped in water to wash down any sugar crystals climbing to the sides of the pan. Continue to boil over high heat, undisturbed, until the mixture turns a rich amber color. Once it turns, you may stir. When it is golden brown (caramelized), remove from the heat. It may smell burned—caramelized sugar literally is burned sugar. Immediately pour the sugar into a 9-inch cake pan at least 3 inches deep, so the sugar coats all sides, or use 8 individual custard cups, well buttered.

¾–1	cup slivered almonds or pine nuts, finely chopped
1	13½-ounce can evaporated milk
1	cup whole milk
1	teaspoon vanilla
3	eggs, beaten
3	egg yolks
¾	cup granulated sugar

Beat together the remaining ingredients. Pour into the prepared pan or cups. Then place in a larger pan, half filled with water. Cover with foil and bake for 55 minutes to 1 hour at 350°, or until the custard is set.

Remove from oven, uncover, and cool out of the water at room temperature 30 minutes. Refrigerate, unmolded and covered, until ready to serve. The sauce will soften during refrigeration. Simply run a knife around the edge and invert to unmold.

▼▼▼

Fonda San Miguel

Variation

You may use pumpkin for an interesting version of this recipe: 1 cup pureed cooked pumpkin, ⅓ cup additional sugar, and 1 teaspoon orange zest.

Storage, Freezing, and Advance Preparation

The flan may be prepared 2 days in advance.

Blue Mesa, *Dallas*   Yield: 10 servings

HONEY FLAN

True to Mexican tradition, Blue Mesa uses honey in many of their desserts. This is very smooth and rich, more like a cream brulee.

4	cups whipping cream
2	teaspoons Mexican vanilla
½	cinnamon stick

Combine the cream, vanilla, and cinnamon stick in a large saucepan and bring to a gentle boil, without scorching. Remove from heat.

5	large eggs
½	cup honey
½	cup sugar

In a separate bowl, beat the eggs, honey, and sugar until smooth. Slowly whisk into the warm cream mixture. Mix well and strain.

½	cup sugar
3	tablespoons water

Heat the sugar and water in a skillet over medium-high heat, without stirring, until the sugar begins to caramelize and turn amber in color. When fully melted, pour about 2 tablespoons into 8-ounce custard cups. Put these in a pan half filled with warm water and fill with the cream mixture. Bake at 350° for about 45 minutes, or until set. Remove and cool.

To serve the flans, run a knife around the edge to loosen the custard and turn upside down. Garnish with fresh berries.

▼▼▼

La Esquina, Dallas   Yield: 6 servings

Praline Dessert

If you are looking for a simple yet impressive dessert, try this combination from La Esquina. Use your favorite pralines and the best-quality ice cream, preferably homemade.

	oil for frying	In a saucepan, bring at least 3 inches of oil to 375° and then, 3 or 4 at a time, fry the tortillas until crisp, browning both sides. This takes just under a minute. Immediately coat with cinnamon sugar.
6	flour tortillas, quartered	
	cinnamon sugar	
1½	quarts vanilla ice cream	Let the ice cream soften enough to allow you to stir the broken pralines throughout it. Refreeze until firm.
10–12	firm pralines, broken	
½	cup Cajeta Sauce (see p. 229) or prepared caramel sauce	Meanwhile, combine the cajeta or caramel sauce with cream, or half-and-half, and Kahlúa. Warm this mixture just prior to serving.
¼	cup heavy cream or half-and-half	
¼	cup Kahlúa	
½–¾	cup whole or slightly broken pecans	Sauté the pecans in butter for several minutes and then drain on paper towels.
2	tablespoons butter	

Assembly and Presentation

Arrange 4 of the tortilla quarters in a serving dish. Place a scoop of ice cream on top, then drizzle with sauce. Top with pecans.

Storage, Freezing, and Advance Preparation

The entire dessert may be prepared in advance and then assembled just prior to serving. I often prescoop the ice cream if serving a large crowd.

Fonda San Miguel, *Austin*

Yield: 8 servings

COFFEE TOFFEE PIE

When garnished with fresh strawberries, dipped in both white and dark chocolate, this creates a beautiful dessert.

The Crust

1	cup all-purpose flour
1	cup walnuts, chopped
1	ounce semisweet chocolate, ground
	dash of salt
1	stick cold butter, cut in 5–6 pieces
1	egg

Using a fork or pastry blender, combine the dry ingredients, cutting in the butter and the egg. Press into a 9-inch pie pan and let rest, refrigerated, 1 to 4 hours.

Prick in several places with a fork and bake at 375° for 12 to 15 minutes or until brown. Cool.

The Filling

1	stick butter
¾	cup brown sugar
1	ounce unsweetened chocolate, melted and cooled
2	teaspoons instant coffee
2	large eggs

Cream the butter and sugar together, then add cooled chocolate and instant coffee. Beat until smooth. Add the eggs 1 at a time. Pour into the cooled crust and refrigerate at least 2 hours until set.

Assembly and Presentation

1	cup whipping cream
2	tablespoons Kahlúa
1	tablespoon powdered sugar
	grated chocolate
	fresh strawberries (optional)

Whip the cream with the Kahlúa and powdered sugar. Mound atop pie and garnish with grated chocolate and fresh strawberries, if desired.

Storage, Freezing, and Advance Preparation

After the filling is poured into the crust, the pie can be frozen and will keep indefinitely.

CHOCOLATE MOUSSE TACOS

There are quite a lot of steps to make this spectacular dessert, but both sauces, the shells, and mousse filling may be made several days in advance. When your friends rave, you'll be sure it was worth the effort. You can fill the shell with ice cream or fresh berries, to cut down on the preparation.

Peach Sauce

1   package frozen peaches, thawed
      sugar to taste

To make the peach and raspberry sauces, blend each separately with sugar to taste, in a blender until smooth. Strain the raspberry sauce. Place each sauce in a plastic "squirt bottle" and refrigerate until ready to use.

Raspberry Sauce

1   package frozen raspberries, thawed
      sugar to taste

Almond Taco Shell

1½ cups sugar
2   cups skinned almonds
⅓ cup milk
½ cup butter

In a food processor fitted with the metal blade, grind the sugar and almonds to a fine powder. Add the milk and butter and mix well. Let the mixture stand for at least 15 minutes.

Transfer the dough to a pastry bag without a tip, and pipe a 3-ounce ball onto a cookie sheet covered with parchment or microwave paper. Press the mound into a thin, round circle about 5 inches in diameter.

▼▼

Blue Mesa

Chocolate Mousse

10	ounces semisweet chocolate chips
6	tablespoons butter
2	egg yolks
2	egg whites
3	tablespoons sugar
2	cups whipping cream

Honey Cream Sauce

2	cups whipping cream
½	cup sugar
½	cup honey

Assembly, Presentation and Garnish

Bake in a 375° oven until evenly browned, about 10–13 minutes. Remove, cutting around the paper and mold around a taco mold or rolling pin to shape. Cookies will harden as they cool.

To make the mousse melt the chocolate in the top of a double boiler. Gradually add butter and stir to combine. Whisk in the egg yolks. Remove from heat and set aside. Beat the egg whites in a separate bowl until stiff. Gradually add sugar and beat until smooth and glossy. Fold into the chocolate mixture. In a chilled bowl, whip the cream until stiff. Fold the chocolate mixture into the cream. Refrigerate until firm, about 3–4 hours.

Place the cream for the sauce into a saucepan and bring to a boil. Cook to reduce the amount of liquid by one-third, about 10 minutes. Add in the sugar and stir to dissolve. Add honey, return to a boil, remove from heat, and strain. Refrigerate until firm, about 3–4 hours.

To assemble, pool the plate with the honey sauce. Using the squirt bottle, make a line of both raspberry and peach sauces on the honey sauce. Draw a knife through the sauces to make a starburst design. Fill the shell with chocolate mousse and place on the sauce. Garnish with a mint sprig or fresh berries.

Yield: 6 servings

PINEAPPLE AND ORANGES TEQUILA

This simple, refreshing dessert is the perfect end to a spicy meal. The fruits may be marinated several days in advance. If you have time, the orange zest is a nice finishing touch.

2	ounces tequila
2	ounces triple-sec
1–2	tablespoons granulated sugar
1	fresh pineapple, peeled, halved, and cored
6	oranges

Combine the marinade ingredients in a glass bowl.

Slice the pineapple and set aside. Using a stripper, remove 12–14 strips of peel from the oranges and set aside. Then, using a sharp knife, cut away the remaining peel and membrane, exposing the orange flesh. Remove sections along the membrane, then squeeze all the juice from the pulp and reserve.

Optional Garnish

strips of orange peel
preserved orange juice
2   tablespoons granulated sugar
granulated or colored sugar

Place both pineapple slices and orange sections in the marinade. Add about ⅓ of the reserved orange juice. Refrigerate, covered, for 3 to 4 hours.

Place strips of orange peel in reserved orange juice and sugar and bring to a boil. Boil for about 3 minutes, then remove and place on waxed paper which is lightly coated with sugar. Roll to coat and then set aside.

When ready to serve, place fruit sections in each bowl. Top with a generous scoop of pineapple sherbet and drizzle juices over the top.

Assembly and Presentation

pineapple sherbet

Garnish with orange zest, if desired, and quartered, fried flour tortillas dredged in cinnamon sugar.

Kokopelli, *Dallas*   Yield: 8–10 servings, 1-9 x 13 pan

CHOCOLATE BREAD PUDDING

When heated, this bread pudding is soft, rich, and very intensely chocolate. At Kokopelli, it is served with a chilled cream anglaise (custard sauce) but you could serve it with vanilla ice cream, whipped cream, or the Tequila Sabayon on page 213.

The Custard

2	cups half and half
1	vanilla bean, split and scraped
1	cup sugar
7	egg yolks

Heat the half and half with vanilla beans and ¾ cup sugar over medium heat just to a simmer. Beat together the egg yolks and remaining sugar until thick. Add about 1 cup of the warm milk, then combine both mixtures and cook over low heat until thickened. Watch the heat carefully so the eggs do not "scramble" or get lumpy. Strain the custard.

1½	pounds semisweet chocolate, melted (about 4 cups)
2	tablespoons unsalted butter

Melt the butter and chocolate together. Whisk in the melted chocolate into the custard and stir until smooth.

¾	pound thinly sliced brioche, or 6 rolls

Cover the bottom of the pan with a thin layer of chocolate, then cover with a layer of thinly sliced brioche. Repeat, making three layers, ending with custard on top. Press down to soak the brioche with chocolate. Cover with foil, place in a larger pan half filled with hot water, and bake at 275° for 50–60 minutes or until the chocolate is set.

Serve the pudding with ice cream or the sauce.

▼▼

Boudro's, *San Antonio*   Yield: 8 servings

Toasted Coconut Custard with Cajeta

Cajeta in Mexico is made from cooking milk and sugar for several hours until it turns a light caramel color. This quick version is just as delicious. You'll find many other uses for this popular sauce.

Cajeta Sauce

1½   cups sugar
½   cup water
2   cups whipping cream or goat's milk
4   ounces butter

To make the sauce, heat the sugar and water over high heat in a large, heavy saucepan. Do not stir. When the sugar begins to caramelize and turns a dark brown color, remove from heat. Add the cream and cook, stirring constantly, until the sauce is smooth and thick. Stir in butter and cool.

Custard

4   cups whole milk
     zest from 1 lime
1   cup powdered sugar
½   cup all-purpose flour
12   egg yolks
2   whole eggs
½   cup Grand Marnier liqueur
1   tablespoon vanilla

Heat the milk over medium-high heat to a simmer. Combine the lime zest, sugar, flour, eggs, egg yolks, Grand Marnier, and vanilla in another saucepan. Gradually add the hot milk to the egg mixture, stirring constantly, over medium-low heat. (Be careful not to scramble the eggs.) Cook until thickened, about 5 minutes. Pour the mixture into a pyrex casserole and cool. Refrigerate until very firm, about 12 hours.

2   beaten eggs
     flour
     unsweetened shredded coconut

Shape the firm custard into logs about 1½ inches high and 5 inches long. Dust with flour, then dip each one first in the beaten eggs and then into shredded coconut.

Boudro's

Heat vegetable oil to about 350°. Fry the logs one at a time until golden brown. (Note: You may find it easier to work with smaller "squares" rather than logs.)

fresh strawberries
mint sprigs

Serve the coconut logs atop warm Cajeta Sauce and garnish with fresh strawberries and a mint sprig.

▼▼

Matt's Ranchero, *Dallas*   Yield: 8–12

Texas Sopaipillas

These are like a cinnamon sugar doughnut rather than the crisp, airy sopaipillas of New Mexico. Matt Martinez takes a shortcut by using the large, refrigerated biscuit dough; however, you can prepare them from any biscuit mix.

Cinnamon Sugar

1½	cups sugar
2	tablespoons ground cinnamon

Combine the cinnamon and sugar in a large bowl and mix well.

The Sopaipillas

2	cups biscuit mix
3	tablespoons sugar
¾	cup whole milk
3–4	cups vegetable or peanut oil

Prepare the biscuit mix with sugar and whole milk according to the package directions and roll out ¼-inch thick on a surface dusted with some of the dry mix. Cover the dough with plastic wrap and let it rest 15 minutes. The dough should be soft but not sticky.

Heat the oil in a deep saucepan to 350–360°. Cut the dough into small triangles. Fry 1 or 2 at a time. Spoon hot oil over the top as they fry. When browned, remove, drain most of the oil, and then put triangles of dough in the bowl of cinnamon sugar and toss to coat.

Hazelnut-Honey Sauce

3	tablespoons butter
¾	cups honey
⅛	cup hazelnut liqueur

Heat the butter, honey, and hazelnut liqueur over medium heat to a simmer.

Matt's Ranchero

Assembly, Presentation and Garnish

vanilla ice cream
fresh seasonal berries

Serve Sopaipillas warm and drizzle with warm honey sauce. Top with vanilla ice cream and garnish with fresh berries.

Advance Preparation

The Sopaipillas may be made ahead and reheated in the microwave for 15–20 seconds before serving.

▼▼

Author's Contribution   Yield: 5 dozen small cookies

MEXICAN NUT COOKIES

These unusual cookies—hollow in the center—are a specialty in many Texas bakeries. They should be light in color, but crisp. Weighing the flour and powdered sugar is essential. I have used pine nuts in place of pecans.

1 cup pine nuts, finely chopped	Toast the nuts on a cookie sheet in a slow oven (275°) for about 12 minutes. Do not brown. Set aside to cool.
6 tablespoons unsalted butter ¾ cup vegetable shortening ½ pound powdered sugar 1 teaspoon vanilla ½ teaspoon almond extract ½ pound cake flour ¼ teaspoon salt	Cream the butter, shortening, and sugar. Add the vanilla, almond extract, flour, salt, and nuts and mix to combine thoroughly.
powdered sugar or cinnamon sugar	Using your hands or a miniature ice cream scoop which has been sprayed with a nonstick vegetable coating, make rounds of dough on very lightly buttered cookie sheets. Bake at 350° for about 12 to 15 minutes. Do not brown. Transfer to wire racks and sift a light coating of sugar over the cookies.

Storage, Freezing, and Advance Preparation

The cookies keep very well, up to 2 weeks.

INDEX